Getaway*X*

Create Wealth and Income with Vacation Real Estate

Trevor Wisniewski

With

Matt Clark
Jonathan Eadie
John T. Frye Jr.
Sandy Gaulin
Gary Herberholz

GetawayInvesting.com, LLC

First Edition

ISBN 978-0-9914129-0-7

e-book ISBN 978-0-9914129-1-4

GetawayInvesting.com, LLC
PO Box 250634
West Bloomfield, MI 48325

www.GetawayInvesting.com

Table of Contents

List of Tables i

List of Figures ii

Disclaimer iii

Preface v

1 Overview 1

A Look Back 2
Traditional Single Family Rentals 5
Horror Stories 7
The Benefits of Vacation Real Estate 8
The Investment 10
My Two Cents 11
Chapter Recap 12

2 Buying a Property 13

DRAW – What Do *You* Want? 14
What To Buy 16
Real Estate Agents 17
Looking At Potential Properties 22

Comparing Properties 24
Timing 27
Income 28
Expenses 33
Break Even Analysis 36
Other Revenue 37
Make an Offer and Negotiate 40
Chapter Recap 42

3 Inspection 45
The Inspection Process 46
The Property Inspector 48
Chapter Recap 50

4 Financing 51
Types of Funding 52
Conforming Loans 52
Non-conforming Loans 52
Portfolio Lending 53
Land Contracts 53
Getting a Loan 54
Application 54
Processing 58
Underwriting 58
Closing 58
Borrowing and Real Estate as an Investment 58
Other Items 61
Chapter Recap 62

5 Insurance 65
Dwelling Limit 66
Contents Insurance 67
Rent Guarantee Insurance 67
Liability Insurance 68
Flood Insurance 68

Other Forms of Insurance 69
Conclusion 69
Chapter Recap 69

6 Legal 71
Legal Protection for Your Investment 72
LLC and Limited Partnership 72
How to Incorporate 73
Maintaining the Corporate Shield 74
Having the Company Own the Property 75
Vacation Rental Restrictions on Use 76
Legal Issues in Renting Your Property 78
The Rental Agreement 80
Conclusion 82
Chapter Recap 82

7 Setting Up Your Business 85
Name Your Business and Property 86
Create Your New Business 86
Website 86
Phone Number 87
Business Address 87
Email 87
Deed 88
Insurance 88
Banking 89
Maintenance 91
Cleaning 93
Property Guide 94
Keys 96
Tracking Your Income and Expenses 98
Check-in and Check-out Procedures 99
Pet Policy 99
Decorating and Furnishings 100
Amenities 104

Supplies Closet 105
Owner's Closet 105
Guest Book 105
Chapter Recap 106

8 Advertising 107
Existing Renters 109
Sales Pitch and Description 109
List of Renters and Prospects 111
Create a Website 113
National and State Focused Advertising Websites 116
Chamber of Commerce and City/Township Websites 117
State Government Websites 117
Property Reviews 117
Flyers and Business Cards 118
Charity Auctions 119
Travel Books/Magazines 119
Niche/Draw 120
Send Out the News! 120
Photos 121
Social Media, Facebook/Twitter 122
Newsletters and Online Blogs 122
Other 122
GetawayX.com 123
Chapter Recap 123

9 Managing the Property 125
Management Companies 126
Do It Yourself 127
Taking Reservations 131
Calling the Renter 133
After Their Stay 134
Rental Agreement 134
Offering Discounts 135

Taking Payments 135
Cancellation Policy 137
Maximum Occupancy, Minimum Nights Stay, and Minimum Age Policies 138
Security Deposits 138
Renter Complaints and Issues 140
Scams 140
Chapter Recap 143

10 Accounting 145
IRS Rules 146
Bookkeeping 148
IRS Passive Activity Rules 149
Chapter Recap 150

11 Website 151
Set Up & Listing 154
Amenities and Photos 154
Rates and Fees 155
Website and Advertising 155
Reservations and Renters 156
Payments 157
Beyond GetawayX 158
Chapter Recap 163

12 Your Own Getaway 'X' 165
Partners 166
Fractional Ownership Properties 167
Multiple Properties 168

About the Authors 169

List of Tables

2.1 Comparison Chart for All Four Condos 27
2.2 Projected Income from Vacation Rental Property 30
2.3 Rates and Dates 32
2.4 Estimated Expenses for Vacation Rental property 35
2.5 Projected Income (non-lake property near the Lakefront Chalet) 38
2.6 Projected Expenses (non-lake property near the Lakefront Chalet) 39

List of Figures

1.1 Your GetawayX Master Mind Group 3

8.1 How to Advertise Your Property 108

9.1 How To Book and Rent Your Vacation Property 128

Disclaimer

This book is not an offer to sell or a solicitation of any investment products, real estate, or other financial product or service. Consult professional assistance for guidance; this book is not a recommendation to invest in real estate. Use this book as a guide. Our results and suggestions in real estate investing do not guarantee your success. Please do your own homework, use your head, and make your own decisions. Buying real estate and renting it out to renters is a risky business. Real estate investing has its risks; do not invest in real estate if you cannot afford to lose your investment. This book is educational, not advisory.

This material is intended for information purposes only and is not intended to apply to any specific situation; and is not intended to create an attorney-client relationship between the author and the reader, or to provide legal advice. It is highly recommended that you consult a qualified attorney near the location of your property to discuss the specifics of any local laws that might affect your rental.

Underwriting guidelines are subject to change, and terms and strategies mentioned here may not be applicable over time. Lenders may have their own underwriting restrictions, known as overlays, which vary based on loan scenarios and circumstances. Each state has its own lending laws, which may not allow for certain strategies described here. The writers recommend that you utilize a Loan Officer who is licensed to lend in the state in which you are purchasing the property.

Please contact your Insurance Agent for current coverage and other underwriting information. For specific terms, conditions, limitations and exclusions of any offered coverage; please refer to the actual policy forms, which may be obtained by your agent.

Preface

This book will guide you, step-by-step, to implement a unique real estate investing strategy. Do you want an awesome vacation home paid for by other people? Do you want more income for your retirement? I am not going to bore you with statistics of the rental market; rather, I will simply tell you that my way works, and this book tells you how to do it. I am not the only author of *Create Wealth and Income with Vacation Real Estate.* I have five co-authors with expertise in the specific areas needed to make this strategy successful.

> Keep this important item in mind: Choosing an investment property is first and foremost a business decision! Do not let your emotions get in the way.

The purpose of this book is to provide a step-by-step method to execute a strategy for investing in vacation real estate. This is a long-run strategy and not a get rich quick scheme, nor is it about flipping real estate. What I outline in this book is a real estate investment business. There is work involved and startup costs to get it up and running. It is not hard, and is actually quite fun. Moreover, it does not take a lot of time: I have a day job and manage our properties in my spare time.

There are a lot of books, publications, and how-to papers on the internet regarding vacation rentals. The industry is extremely fragmented, and websites and resources are scattered all over the internet. Until now, there was no all-encompassing how-to book, and no central website, with all the resources you need to implement this strategy.

Throughout this book I will reference two of my properties. The first is a cottage located in Northern Michigan on an all-sports lake nestled in the middle of the Manistee National forest, which I call the "Up North Getaway," or the "Lakefront Chalet." The second property is a condo at the base of a popular ski hill in Northern Michigan, referred to as the "Boyne Mountain Getaway," or the "Ski Condo."

A vacation property does not have to be expensive.

Your first thought might be, "How in the world can I afford the down payment on a vacation home?" Simply put, the expense is relative. For example, my Ski Condo cost $300,000; it is a five-bedroom, five-bath, three-level condo sitting directly on the ski slope. It is a very large condo situated in the area's premier location. If I could not afford to buy this property, but still really wanted to buy in the area, there are smaller slope-side condos on the same ski hill for around $100,000.

The Lakefront Chalet cost $269,000 and is a three-bedroom plus loft, three-bath, three-level chalet sitting on 165 feet of an all-sports lake. Again, this property is in a premier location. If I did not want to spend that much money, but I still wanted to buy in the area, there are many homes not on the lake that cost under $100,000. My point here is that if you really love an area and want to buy a vacation home there, look at all of your options. If you cannot afford your "dream vacation home" right now, but you still want to buy a vacation home, look around in the area – you should be able to find a property that you can afford. Sure, it might not be directly on the beach, ski hill, or lake, but as long as you are in the area, you should be able to rent it to vacationers.

For the purposes of illustration, I will primarily use examples of higher-end vacation homes throughout this book. For example, there will be sample income and expense numbers for our Ski Condo, and a comparison of four condos on the beach in Florida. One exception is a reference to a much less expensive property that is near our Lakefront Chalet.

All of the tools and resources to execute this plan are on my website, and they are all free. Go to GetawayX.com and create a login and password; there you can download, edit, and print many of the resources mentioned in this book. Make sure to login as a "Property Owner" not as a renter.

Now, let's get started so that you, too, can have your own Getaway 'X'!

Chapter 1

Overview

What you will learn . . .

- Surround yourself with knowledgeable people
- The difference between traditional single-family rentals and vacation rentals
- Vacation property as an investment

. . . and more!

A Look Back

When I graduated from college in 1991, my best friend and I got our first real-world jobs. It didn't take long for us to realize that our day jobs were not going to make us rich. Real estate intrigued both of us and, heck, back then people like Donald Trump always talked about real estate as the way to make a lot of money. I'm sure you've heard it from someone you know . . . "Buy land! They don't make any more of it." We decided to read a few books and then decide where to go from there. The two books we agreed to read cover-to-cover were, *Think and Grow Rich* by Napoleon Hill, and *Creating Wealth* by Robert Allen. If you haven't read them already, I highly recommend these books.

Think and Grow Rich will get you motivated. In it we learned about the "Master Mind group": surrounding yourself with competent people. Your Master Mind group are the people who will motivate you, assist you, and provide advice and guidance along the way. To make this strategy work, it is extremely important to have a competent group of people around you. You may partner with someone – your best friend or your spouse – when buying your first property. You will need to divide the work and duties based on your strengths, and you must be able to get along in good times and in bad. In addition, you will need a good accountant, marketing partners (i.e., advertising websites), an attorney, a handyman, a cleaning person, contractors, this book, and a real estate agent, among others. See Figure 1.1 below: these people are your Master Mind group.

Think and Grow Rich teaches the technique of goal setting, which correlates directly to success. The author suggests that you write out your goals and put them in front of you, so that you are forced to see them every day. This seemed like a simple, logical thing to do, so I did it. I had personal and professional goals. I typed them all out and hung them in my cubicle at work. My co-workers would occasionally stop by my cubicle, read some of my goals, and make jokes about them. I really didn't mind because I was on a mission – a mission to succeed

Figure 1.1: Your GetawayX Master Mind Group

at many things. Among my personal goals were skydiving, climbing a glacier, and bungee jumping. Those, along with the goal to be CEO of the company I worked for, got the most laughs.

Well, I accomplished most of those goals. However, I soon realized that the corporate world wasn't for me, and I deleted the CEO goal. When I led a big software project that reduced head count and made our client's operation much more efficient, it was estimated that well over a million dollars per year would be saved. My boss was extremely happy with me, and the project came in under budget and ahead of schedule. (Yes, those were on my goals list as well, posted in my cube.) He called me into his office and told me that he had fought hard and had gotten me a whopping $3,000 bonus for my great performance, and for the millions

I had saved. The math didn't add up! I concluded that if I wanted to be rich, this wasn't the way to do it. As a result, I followed one of my other goals: buy single-family homes and rent them out to make money.

Robert Allen has many books on real estate, and in the 1990s I read *Creating Wealth* and *Nothing Down for the 90s*. Through his books I learned how to buy real estate with nothing down, and many other creative techniques to inexpensively buy real estate. At that time I was a kid right out of college and I didn't have money to buy anything, let alone a house. In this book I won't discuss how to creatively buy real estate with nothing down, because there are many books on the topic of creative financing by authors like Robert Allen. Even if you end up buying a vacation home with a traditional 20% down mortgage, it is helpful to know these creative buying techniques. At any time you may encounter the right seller with whom a creative technique will pay off big time.

After reading these books I purchased my first single family home, borrowing money from my parents. In the early 1990s the rate on my 30-year 3% down loan was 9%. The house was a cute little three bedroom, one bath bungalow in Ferndale, Michigan. I paid $55,000 for it and rented it for $750 per month. I had a positive cash flow and was excited, because this actually worked! The renters took care of the home and paid promptly every month. I thought, "Wow, this is easy." About six months into their rental, my renters told me they were going to move out because they wanted to buy their own house. That should have been my first red flag, but I thought, oh well, this probably happens.

Fast-forward ten years and my buddy and I had bought and sold well over 25 homes, and had invested in everything from a mobile home to single-family homes, condos, and vacant land. We both had normal day jobs, and did this after work and on the weekends. We bought and sold properties with many creative techniques: nothing down, lease-with-option, seller's concessions, land contract, and the conventional way with a mortgage and a down payment. We did buy-fix-up flips, buy-rent-and-hold, and we did a spec home. After all the headaches, we decided to get out of the business, and between 1999 and 2002, we sold all of our properties.

Traditional Single Family Rentals

We just couldn't take it anymore. Being a landlord to full-time renters wore us out. By this time we were both married and had families, and time spent with family was more valuable than fixing a leaky pipe at our rental houses, or dealing with renter issues. As for the headaches, where do I start? First off, most municipalities require a "Landlord's License" when renting a single family home. If you have to evict a renter and don't have the license, the courts will not hear your case, and will fine you if you are renting the property without a license.

Dealing with yearly city inspections wasn't fun. Every year new items to fix or improve were cited, even though the house didn't change from one year to the next. On average, $500 to $2000 per home was required each year to comply with the terms of the landlord license. Additionally, once rented out, you then had to chase your renters around every month for rent. I know a landlord who sent a thirty-day notice of eviction to every one of his renters at the beginning of every month. This sped up the eviction time for him in case they didn't pay; and if they paid, the notice became legally null and void. The notices frightened the renters enough to pay.

Think about it! Your renters live in your rental home every day of the year, creating a lot of wear and tear on the home, inside and out. Renters do not take care of the property as you would, because they don't own it. And when they move out, the property must be fixed or repaired to rent back out again, which can cost a lot of money.

Dealing with renters' complaints was draining and constant. My experience was that renters noticed everything and complained about everything. Collecting the monthly rent was one of our hardest tasks. I heard every excuse under the sun as to why renters didn't have the money to pay their monthly rent. Evicting renters who didn't pay was painful, as well as a big pain in the wallet, and it happened more often than not. Eventually, many good paying renters fell on hard times and stopped paying their rent

Landlords must follow a specific eviction process, and it takes about sixty days to finally get them out of your house. By that time, they hate you and think you are the devil. Evicted renters think their failure to pay rent is your fault and not theirs, and they end up trashing your house. This happened to us many times. Any seasoned landlord will tell you that the key to having a good renter in a single-family home is selecting the right renters in the first place. This is true; however, we learned that this rule wasn't always applicable.

For example, we had a nice three bedroom, two-story home in a nice suburb of Detroit, which we bought as a VA repo back in the early 1990s. Being immature cocky kids, we bid $69,069.69 on it and won. We wanted to make sure that our bid was noticed. Anyway, we screened many renters and finally rented it to three young adults who had just graduated college, all of them having new jobs in the Detroit area. These were perfect renters who paid every month, on time, and had good credit, good jobs, and were good people. However, just as we experienced with our first house in Ferndale, these qualities also made them the worst renters. After their one-year lease expired, they had all saved enough money and built up enough credit to buy their own homes.

Long story short: when you own single-family rentals you are renting to people who can't buy a house for whatever reason, or they wouldn't be renting from you. You end up renting to people who don't care about you, your house, or paying you on time. To my renters, the rental situation was always us against them, no matter how much I bent over backwards to accommodate them. I could feel it and see it in their eyes.

Horror Stories

As an investor I have bought, sold, flipped, and rented properties for over 20 years – and it wasn't all bad. There were a few good renters, and at times things went okay. In saying that, I would like to share with you some horror stories from my traditional single-family rentals, and from other landlords I know.

After evicting one of our renters, we noticed an extremely large dog living in the house. We called the police, got the dog removed, and noticed that the animal had pooped everywhere. The drywall was ripped off the bathroom walls, and the house was filled with fleas. Out in the back yard, it appeared that the renter never picked up any of the dog's poop. Most of the grass was dead, and the yard was a disgusting mess.

Inspecting another home that renters had recently left, we were greeted by a pile of human feces in the center of the living room, sex toys and sex paraphernalia in the attic (alongside a nasty mattress), a broken-down minivan in the back yard, and the frame of a car in the garage. The police had to tag the cars before we could do anything with them.

After evicting non-paying renters, a friend of mine went to his house and found several five gallon buckets of human waste on the back porch. He noticed that there was an issue with the plumbing, and because the renters had not been paying their rent, they hadn't wanted to call the landlord. Apparently, they had taken matters into their own hands.

Maybe you're saying to yourself that these are just low-income "slumlord" homes. Well, I know someone very close to me who had similar issues renting a $350,000 four bedroom, 3,000 square foot home, including threats of lawsuits from his renters. The point is that you are dealing with a renter who LIVES in the home you own. In stark contrast, *over the past twelve years of renting vacation properties, I have had no horror stories because the renters vacation at the property, they don't live there.*

Don't get me wrong – we have had a few small issues over the past decade, but these have primarily involved overenthusiastic renters enjoying their vacation at our property a little too much, thus irritating the neighbors.

> I was able to learn from what I did correctly, and from the mistakes I made. I have learned what to do and what not to do. After over twenty years of real estate investing experience, and after buying millions of dollars of real estate, I strongly recommend the vacation property rental over the single-family rental in order to create wealth via real estate.

The Benefits of Vacation Real Estate

Before I tell you about the benefits of vacation real estate, keep in mind that you will be a real estate owner of a home or a condo, and things can and will go wrong. It's just part of real estate investing. However, the GetawayX.com website has a list of suggested maintenance steps that will help you to avoid big problems.

Let's talk now about the benefits of vacation rentals over traditional rentals. People who rent vacation homes can afford a vacation, and PRE-PAY in advance of their stay at your property. They are also looking forward to their vacation and are generally in a great mood. They tend to take very good care of your property. Some of my renters have actually left me notes on little things they fixed, because they loved staying in our properties so much. Moreover, the wear and tear on your vacation property is minimal. Think of how much time you spend in a hotel room on vacation. For the most part you are there to sleep, and during the day you are out and about enjoying your vacation. Renters in vacation rentals leave a small footprint because they are renting for a weekend or week at a time. Vacationers don't have much time to trash the place and they don't spend a lot of time there – they are on vacation, not renting your property to sit around the house all day.

Vacation rentals can be a bigger bang for your buck. One of my vacation rental properties is worth about $300,000. I would need six normal, single-family rental homes that cost about $50,000 each to equal one vacation property at $300,000. That's right: six of my old single-family homes I once owned equal one of my vacation rentals. That's five fewer properties to worry about, five fewer headaches, five fewer sets of renters, five fewer roofs, five fewer furnaces, five fewer places to maintain, and five fewer groups to collect monthly rent from.

You have heard that real estate is all about location, which is 100 percent true. Which would you rather have completely paid off in retirement: six single-family rentals in a suburb of a large metropolitan city, or a lakefront chalet in a beautiful vacation destination? Which do you think will have more value, and be more desirable? Upon retirement, would you still want to run around and collect monthly rents from those six homes in the suburbs, or would you rather be renting one lakefront chalet and routinely vacationing there?

There are many benefits to renting vacation properties versus traditional single-family rentals.

In renting single-family homes I learned that even in a great economy I still had bad renters, because those renters who were doing well could afford to buy their own homes. I was stuck with people who could not afford their own home. In a bad economy I also had bad renters, and everyone had excuses for not making the rent. Therefore, a good economy or a bad economy equals problems with single-family rentals. I was worried when I bought our first vacation rental in the summer of 2001.

I was concerned because September 11th changed the world we lived in, and I wondered if people would still vacation as they did in the past. I was also very concerned in 2008 and 2009 when the stock market fell, and the economy and real estate went to hell. However, in both circumstances, my rentals were not affected at all. Whether the economy is good or bad, vacation rentals are still good for the property owner. It seems that no matter what is going on in the world or in the economy, people still go on vacation. That's because you are targeting people who have the money to vacation. These people look forward to their vacations, appreciate them, and can afford them.

Do you have a plan to save money and buy your dream vacation home in retirement? Well, don't wait until retirement to do it! Why not start now and generate rental income to help pay for the property? And better yet, YOU get to use the property every year. I cannot tell you how many family memories have been created from our time at our vacation homes.

The Investment

Let's take a look at this method of real estate investing. You could apply what you learn in this book, buy a vacation property at a good price, rent it to cover all of your costs, and have positive cash flow each year. But for me it is not about making yearly income right now; it is about creating wealth and creating an income stream in the future. To illustrate this, here is an example of an expensive vacation property that has negative cash flow each year.

Let's say that you purchase a property for $300,000 and put 10% down ($30,000) on a 30-year mortgage. Now, assume that each year after income and expenses there is a loss of $2,000 per year. In 30 years the property will be paid off and you will have "lost" $60,000 renting it during the period of the mortgage (30 years * −$2,000 per year = −$60,000). Therefore, the property will cost you a total of $90,000 ($30,000 + $60,000) over the life of the mortgage.

Recall that you "lost" $2,000 per year on the property. But you have also used it as a vacation home for 30 years! The $2,000 per year you "lost" is most likely less than what it would have cost you to vacation every year. You now have an investment property worth (in 2014 dollars) $300,000, for which you spent $90,000. If you sold the property you would make $210,000, a 233% rate of return. And that is in 2014 dollars: chances are that in 30 years the property will be worth more than $300,000. I estimate the 20-year average rate of appreciation for real estate to be around 4%. That means in 30 years the property would be worth over $900,000, not $300,000!

You bought this property to use as a vacation home, and for an income stream in retirement. Let's say it brings in $20,000 per year in net income, which equals a 22% rate of return on your initial investment of $90,000. Your $90,000 pays you $20,000 per year in retirement! Not bad for one property, and in retirement you can still use it for a vacation home for your family. But that is underestimating the value of rental income 30 years from now. I have seen many numbers on averages for rental rates, but I estimate the 20-year average rate of rental appreciation for real estate to be around 3%. This means that in 30 years the property would be generating over $48,000 in rental income every year, not $20,000 per year: a yearly return of over 50% on your investment!

That is why I love this method of real estate investing. You get a place to vacation AND make money doing it.

My Two Cents

I have a day job, and all of my real estate investing has been on the side. Although I have made millions of dollars over the past 20 years as a stock and options trader, my preferred investment for my personal money has always been real estate. Yes, you heard it correctly. I live and breathe the stock market every day of my working life, and I prefer my personal money to be in real estate – not stocks, not gold, not FOREX. I watch CNBC every day of the week and for every "expert" on TV telling me to buy gold, there is another "expert" telling me to sell gold. The same goes for stocks. I have no idea what the value of gold or a certain stock will be fifteen or thirty years from now, but I can tell you that my properties will be paid off by then. Not only paid off, but paid off by my rental income, not my personal income. And I can tell you my projected yearly income from my real estate fifteen or thirty years from now. Sure, the value of the actual real estate will fluctuate; it could be worth more or less than it is now, but that is not the only reason I am investing. I can go to my properties and touch them; they are physical structures in desirable vacation areas. The Ski Condo is on one of the most popular ski hills in Michigan, and in an area where no more properties can be developed – what's there is what will still be there decades from now.

> The past twelve years of investing in vacation real estate has been fun and enjoyable. In the future, when all of my vacation properties are paid off, I would rather own awesome property in places where I love to vacation, instead of owning full-time single family homes in the middle of the suburbs of big cities!

Chapter Recap

- If your goals are to create an income stream, or to create long-term wealth, get that dream vacation home now and have other people help you pay for it.
- Set your goals and keep them in front of you!
- Surround yourself with a group of knowledgeable people that will help you achieve your goals.
- The benefits of vacation rental property far outweigh those of traditional single-family rentals.

Chapter 2

Buying a Property

What you will learn . . .

- What are YOU looking for?
- Real estate agents: how to select one and what to tell them
- What to do while looking at potential properties, and how to compare them
- How to calculate the projected income, expenses, and the break-even analysis

. . . and more!

> Choosing what property to buy as an investment is first and foremost a business decision! Do not let your emotions get in the way.

Most real estate books will tell you to always buy low and sell high, but in my system you don't have to worry about missing low mortgage interest rates and inexpensive real estate prices. Of course it is very good if you can get into real estate near the bottom of the market, but in the long run, it really doesn't matter. My most recent vacation rental was bought at a ten-year price low, and the mortgage rate was at its lowest level in years. That is awesome, the perfect storm. But again, it really doesn't matter – the math just has to work. I bought my first rental house in 1992 with a 9% mortgage, and I still had positive monthly cash flow from it. Our first vacation rental, the Lakefront Chalet, was purchased in 2001, which was the top tick for real estate prices in Michigan. Today it is worth about the same as what I paid for it. However, yearly rentals have paid down the mortgage to the point where I now owe much less than what it's currently worth, and the property generates a nice rental income.

DRAW – What Do *You* Want?

First and foremost, you must know what you are going to use the vacation home for, and then determine if you are able to rent it. Remember, you and your family will be spending time at the property now and in retirement, so it has to be what you want! I wanted a place one hour's drive time from my favorite fishing streams and lakes. My wife and I like to ski in the winter and ride jet skis in the summer. Northwest Michigan has all of this to offer; but now I had to zero in on a specific area.

In real estate it's all about location, just as everyone says. Ask yourself what will draw people to pay you money to vacation at your property, and what draw will maximize your rental income? It is best when people have multiple reasons to want to rent your property. To get the most rental income from your property, you should also consider what the area has to offer year round.

Remember this: the attractions that draw people to vacation at your home should all be within a one-hour drive from the property. Most people on vacation will drive 30 minutes to an hour on day-trips, but any farther than that is a stretch. There are many tourist activities within an hour from our Lakefront Chalet, which makes it a great central point for a vacation. And don't forget the intangibles . . . many people simply want a secluded place away from the big city.

> You may already have some favorite vacation places and would love to own a vacation property there. Keep in mind that not all vacation areas will meet your break-even number. You must first determine the math and rental feasibility before wasting a lot of your time.

Not all vacation properties are expensive. In most states you can buy a nice little home near a lake for a very reasonable amount of money, and rent it as a vacation home. You don't have to be right on the water. Several vacation rentals near our Lakefront Chalet are not on the lake, but are consequently much cheaper, and charge renters less than we do. It is all relative: draw and location will demand more rental income, but will also come with a more expensive price tag.

Back in 2000, I decided to investigate vacation homes in Northern Michigan. My father had been taking me up to that area since I was a kid, and I always had a dream to buy a place up there. My initial plan was to buy 20 or 40 acres of land, and buy a trailer to put on the property. I looked at a lot of properties, and I could have bought a 40 acre parcel with a trailer for about $50,000. It was very enticing until I talked it over with my family. My wife and my mom informed me that they would never use such a property, and it would be just for me and my dad. My dad and I chuckled: we thought there was nothing wrong with that! But reality set in . . . I was married and obviously had other people to consider. So I came up with a better idea. How about buying something really nice (my dream vacation home) and renting it out to cover all or most of the costs? That way, I could purchase something our entire family could use year-round.

But that idea would cost a lot more than $50,000. I had all the normal reservations: could I afford the extra mortgage? How could I realistically afford a second home? Who was going to mow the lawn and fix everything that breaks? To top it off, one of the real estate investing books I read years ago said to never buy rental property over one hour away from your home, because it would be hard to manage. The only thing going for me was my many years of experience renting single-family homes in the Detroit suburbs. After thinking it over, I decided to take the risk and see how it would go.

> I didn't realize it at the time, but I had just stumbled upon the best way to invest in real estate!

What To Buy

Do you prefer condos or houses? I own both and love both. In the past I had always preferred a house over a condo, but after owning a condo for a couple years, I began to see its benefits. Now I wouldn't care if my next vacation rental was a house or a condo. I have heard other vacation condo owners say that condos are much easier to manage from a long distance, but I have not found that to be true. Whether your property is a condo or a house, managing them is the same. The main difference in management is the exterior maintenance. The exterior maintenance of a condo is taken care of for you (yard work, snow removal, and so on). You have to hire someone to do this for you if you own a house. But once you hire someone, they do it like clockwork and just send you a bill – it's not that hard to manage. That's why managing a condo isn't a major time saver. Another difference between a condo and a house are the amenities that come with a condo: tennis courts, pool, hot tub, golf course, health club, spa, water park; the list goes on. The downside of a condo is paying the monthly HOA fees, special assessments that may arise, and the association's rules that you and your renters must follow.

Whether to buy a condo or a house will be partly decided by your personal preferences, and partly by what kinds of properties are in the area. In our Ski Condo development, homes can go for over a million dollars, but the condos are much more affordable and easier to rent. If I didn't like condos, I would never have bought in that area because I wouldn't have been able to afford other properties. When I looked at beachfront property in Florida, the only properties in my price range were condos, and I had no choice but to look at condos. When I looked for our Lakefront Chalet, the area contained houses only and no condos, so buying a house was the way to go. The area in which you are looking will most likely play a big factor in what type of property you will buy – you might not have a choice.

Real Estate Agents

Back in the early 2000s, my business partner and I wanted to sell our single-family rental homes. Back then, neither of us had a very favorable view of real estate agents. We viewed them as people who were in it for themselves and who just wanted a quick sale to collect a commission. We had numerous houses to sell, and we didn't want to pay a 6% commission to an agent for just putting the listings on the MLS, and getting a purchase agreement from another agent. Back then we couldn't see the value added. We decided that one of us should get a real estate license and sell them ourselves on the MLS through a broker, thus saving us thousands of dollars in commissions. However, neither of us had the time to study for and take the test. We played rock-paper-scissors, and I lost: I had to take the real estate licensing exam. After passing the exam I joined a large national real estate firm and have held an active real estate license with them ever since. Even though I have never practiced real estate sales as a full time job, the license helped me and my partner to unload all of our rental homes. Over the years I have helped family and friends buy and sell their homes on the side.

Losing that bet was a blessing in disguise. My view of real estate agents has dramatically changed, and now I truly respect the profession. People never see the work involved behind the scenes that ensures a deal goes smoothly. Through the years I have learned a lot about the real estate sales industry. Choose your agent wisely because this process can take some time, and you and your agent must have a great relationship and be patient with each other.

Once you have an idea where you want to buy, you should begin your search. I selected an area from Manistee to Cadillac, Michigan, and went online to start my search. Using Yahoo!, Google, Zillow, Trulia, Bing, and other search engines, you will find properties for sale and real estate agencies in the area in which you are looking.

Before contacting a real estate agent, look closely at the properties you have found online. Are there properties that interest you? Can you afford what you want? Once you have a better idea what you want to buy and can afford, contact a local real estate agent in that area, but don't use just any agent who answers the phone. When you call the real estate agency you should look for one of the following (in order):

1. An agent who comes personally referred to you by someone you trust.
2. An agent with the designation of "Resort & Second Home Property Specialist."
3. One of the top sales agents in the office.
4. An agent who has many years of experience helping buyers purchase a vacation home.

Before wasting a lot of your time and the agent's time, ask the agent about Rental Feasibility – is short-term renting allowed in the area where you want to buy? If so, are there any restrictions on renting the property? Do you need a rental license from the city or township?

When we looked at buying an oceanfront condo in Florida, the real estate agent told us that some condo buildings do not allow you to rent at all, some require a minimum of one month rentals, others a two-week minimum, and others only rent by the week, but with no weekend rentals. The condo I bought on Mackinac Island in Michigan is located downtown, and there is a strict rental restriction whereby you can only rent by the month. On the island that means only June through August. Restrictions like these can dramatically affect the break-even number on your investment. If you are buying a condo, you or your real estate agent can easily check with the condo association for any rental restrictions. This becomes a little more difficult when buying a house. First ask your real estate agent if it is legal to rent the home as a vacation property. Call the local city or township and talk with them; verify that it is okay to rent your property to vacationers on a short term basis. You might even be required to get a permit or rental license from the city or township.

As an investor, the real estate agent you choose will make this process easy, or very difficult. There are many competent agents out there, but buying a home that is at least four hours away from where you live creates more work for you and your agent. You will need to rely on your agent for a lot more than just looking at properties. You will need their advice on the area, pricing your rentals, maintenance person contacts, cleaning person contacts, financing contacts, and their professional opinion on the market you are buying into. Your agent must have experience in your target area, and experience buying real estate as a rental investment.

If an agent works for you as a buyer's agent, you may be required to sign a document stating your relationship with the agent. But please note, unless required in your state, you do not need to sign anything with an agent to have them show you properties for sale. If the agent insists that you sign a buyer's agency form, I recommend you sign it for 1) the specific property you are looking at, or 2) if the real estate agent wants a timeframe, sign on with them for a week or up to a month. Years ago, I had an agent in Chicago insist that I sign a six-month buyer's agency agreement with her before she would show me any properties. This would have required me to use her exclusively, even if she and I didn't work out, for six months. You need to feel your real estate agent out, and they need to feel you out. It might be that after a few days of showings, you both might not want to work with each other. When you find the right real estate agent, they will have patience and bend over backwards to help you find your vacation property, and most likely without signed documents locking you to them for months at a time.

> A few notes on "Agency." Agency is how you are being represented in a real estate transaction. I recommend that you find an agent who will represent you as your "Buyer's Agent."

That means that when you make an offer on a property, your agent represents you and only you in the deal, and works solely on your behalf. If you were to call an agent off a sign in the front yard of a property, that agent is a "Seller's Agent" and works for the best interest of the seller, not you. The seller's agent would also love to work with you as well, and would want to create a "Dual Agency," representing both you and the seller in the transaction. I never understood how that can realistically work, though – it is similar to one attorney who works for both the prosecution and the defense at the same time. This never made sense to me, and rightfully so, because in a dual agent arrangement, the agent cannot provide a lot of guidance to either party involved; otherwise the agent would be breaching their duties as agent for the other party. Long story short, you wouldn't get a ton of help from the agent in a

Dual Agency relationship. Try to find a great agent who will work for you and be your buyer's agent.

Once you have contacted a real estate agent in the area where you're looking to buy, have a heart-to-heart conversation with them. As I mentioned earlier, the agent must be experienced in helping people buy vacation/second homes as an investment. Next, you must provide them with the following information. If they balk at any of this, find a different real estate agent.

- Let the agent know that you are buying a vacation property and renting it to vacationers, and that if the math doesn't work, you will not buy the property. Plain and simple. The agent must know that this is a business purchase, not an emotional one.
- Let the agent know what type of draw(s) you are looking for: ocean view, lakefront, riverfront, ski hill, fishing, acreage, or whatever it is you desire for your vacation home.
- Let the agent know what geographical area you want to buy in.
- The agent must understand the maximum amount you are willing to pay.
- Inform the agent about the size and type of property you are interested in (i.e., five bedroom, five bath condo, or three bedroom, two bath house).
- Tell the agent that your process could take a while. Unless you know exactly where you want to buy, executing this plan could take a couple of years. It took me one year to find our Lakefront Chalet, and two years to find and buy the Ski Condo.

Remember, real estate agents are in the business of sales. If the agent gets pushy or is really pressing you hard to make an offer on a property, remind them of your heart-to-heart talk. If the agent doesn't change, choose a different agent. A good real estate agent will provide you with a lot of assistance, as well as their experience in buying your investment property. A good agent will try hard to make your purchase a successful one, not pressure you into buying a property.

Looking At Potential Properties

At this point you know the type of draw and the area in which you want to buy. You have also checked the rental feasibility and have a real estate agent. The next step is to start looking at properties! You have to buy the property for what you want – the draw, and what the area has to offer you while vacationing. Don't get wrapped up in the décor; paint and carpet can be easily changed, but you can't create lakefront living if you buy in the middle of a forest. Ensure that your property is in the location you want, in an area that can easily be rented because of the draws, and understand what the area has to offer vacationers.

The vacation property should have what people expect in that area for rentals. If vacationers renting in the area expect a hot tub, make sure to buy a unit with a hot tub – or get one installed after your purchase. Call local management companies and ask them what types of properties rent best (condos or houses), and the top five amenities renters most desire and ask for. You may already know the answers to these questions if you are buying in an area where you have been vacationing.

When previewing potential properties, take a notepad and pen, and make a list of fix-up costs. Keep track of improvements and fix-ups needed to get the property in shape to rent. This is an area where my spouse and I complement each other. I am the logical math guy who loves to crunch the numbers. My wife's strong point is design and décor. While looking at potential properties, I ask her if she would stay there, and if not, why not? What must be changed to get her to rent the place? Having another eye is invaluable, because alone you might not catch everything on your quick walk through the property. Sometimes you don't have to change much if renters in the area expect what is already there.

> As you walk through each property, keep a detailed list, by room, of everything that must be cleaned, repaired, replaced, or is missing that you will need to buy.

If there are no appliances, for example, you must buy them before renting the property. Establish a cost for each of the items on your list. While walking through the properties, compare the condition of each one to the others. You do not have to make your place the absolute best vacation property known to man. Rather, you must make it competitive and comparable to other vacation rental properties in the area. If most properties in the area haven't been updated since 1980, then you might not HAVE to spend a lot updating it. However, if all of the units are updated and you see one you like that was last updated in 1980, you will likely have to update it in order to be competitive with the other properties. The bright side is that you will probably be able to buy the outdated one much cheaper than the updated ones. If the price is right, the property might be worth buying and renovating.

This brings me to fixer-uppers, which can be diamonds in the rough, and if bought on the cheap, can provide a big bang for your buck. However, there are some things to keep in mind when buying a fixer-upper vacation property.

Buying a property that needs a lot of work requires down-time for renovation, which could cause a lack of rental income while it's being renovated. If you choose this route, time your purchase and renovations to occur during the "off-peak" season. Another drawback is that you have to manage your renovations from a distance – potentially a very long distance – which could be difficult. It's not impossible but you must think creatively, and do it a little differently than if you were updating a home you live in. Over the years we have vastly renovated our Lakefront Chalet with minimal issues.

We do not use the cheapest contractors. We go with a reputable company that has been around for years, and is still in the business of renovating homes. This way we trust that they are more reputable, and will better manage the project. We had the contractor take pictures of the work at the end of every other day or so, and text/email the pictures to us so that we could check on the renovation progress from far away. We also made a couple of visits to check on the progress and meet with the contractor. If you decide to go this route, put a good plan in place with your contractors to make sure you are involved as much as you desire.

Comparing Properties

Now that you have seen some potential properties to buy, it is time to compare them by the numbers.

> To easily compare properties by the numbers, take the asking price and adjust it by (a) adding/subtracting the value of the draw, and (b) adding/subtracting the condition of the house. Next, simply divide your adjusted asking price by the square footage of the property. This will give you the "price per square foot."

Let's say you find two properties: one is directly on the beach overlooking the ocean, and the other is a few blocks away from the beach with no views of the ocean. The beachfront condo is completely renovated and the off-beach condo needs some work. To make the comparison easy, we'll say that both properties are two-bedroom, two-bath condos with 1,200 square feet.

- Condo #1. The renovated beachfront condo price is $250,000.
- Condo #2. The fixer-upper off-beach condo price is $130,000.

After talking to the real estate agent, you discover that beachfront condos cost on average $100,000 more than comparable condos not directly on the beach. The value of being directly on the beach is the beachfront "draw." Additionally, you estimate that it will cost $45,000 to fix-up the off-beach condo and make it as nice as the beachfront condo.

Which condo is a better deal? At first glance you might think that the off-beachfront condo is better because it is priced far below the beachfront one. But let's look at the math.

To compare them we will first subtract the value of the draw. Therefore, if the beachfront condo wasn't on the beach it should sell for $150,000 ($250,000 – $100,000). So $150,000 is the value of a completely renovated off-beach condo (Condo #1). Next, we projected $45,000 to fix up the off-beach condo. Add $45,000 to the price of the off-beach condo ($130,000 + $45,000) for a value of $175,000 (Condo #2). By doing this simple math, you can easily see that the fixer-upper off-beach condo is overpriced (175k vs. 150k).

Now use this information to your advantage. Say, for example, you are interested in buying the fixer-upper off-beach condo that lists for $130,000. Provide your real estate agent with your simple math analysis to justify offering the seller a much lower price. In this case the fixer-upper off-beach condo should sell for $105,000, because $105,000 plus the $45,000 fix up cost equals $150,000, which is the value of the completely renovated off-beach condo.

The above example made it easy to compare two condos of the same size, but how often will that happen? Realistically, the properties you will be comparing will not be identical. We need to take the math one step further, computing the price per square foot. Once you have the math computed as above, simply divide your new adjusted price by the square footage of the property. This will give you the "price per square foot," which will place all of the properties on a level playing field.

Let's continue with our analysis and add two more properties: a beachfront two-bedroom, two-bath condo with 1,000 square feet for $220,000 (aka Condo #3), and an off-beach two-bedroom, two-bath condo with 900 square feet for $120,000 (aka Condo #4). Both condos are completely renovated and do not need any fix ups.

Condo #1 = 1,200 square foot renovated beachfront condo. ADJUSTED price is $150,000 ($250,000 – $100,000).

Condo #2 = 1,200 square foot fixer-upper off-beach condo. ADJUSTED price is $175,000 ($130,000 + $45,000).

Condo #3 = 1,000 square foot renovated beachfront condo. ADJUSTED price is $120,000 ($220,000 – $100,000 draw).

Condo #4 = 900 square foot renovated off-beach condo. Price is $120,000.

The price per square foot comparison:

Condo #1 = $150,000 / 1,200 square feet = $125 per square foot.

Condo #2 = $175,000 / 1,200 square feet = $145 per square foot.

Condo #3 = $120,000 / 1,000 square feet = $120 per square foot.

Condo #4 = $120,000 / 900 square feet = $133 per square foot.

As you can see, the size of the property plays a big role in determining what it should sell for. At first glance Condo #4 is the cheapest fully renovated condo, priced at $120,000. However, based strictly on the math, Condo #3 is the best buy at $120 per square foot.

These general examples show you how to compare properties, and what they should sell for. Every area is unique and you will have to adjust your analysis based on how that area values a draw, and what constitutes a draw. A condo complex directly on the beach with ocean views has more than the obvious draws of beachfront and ocean view. In a

Table 2.1: Comparison Chart for All Four Condos

Property	Asking Price	Draw	Fix-ups	Adjusted Price	Square Feet	Price per Sq. Foot
Condo#1	$250,000	-$100,000	$0	$150,000	1,200	$125
Condo#2	$130,000	$0	$45,000	$175,000	1,200	$145
Condo#3	$220,000	-$100,000	$0	$120,000	1,000	$120
Condo#4	$120,000	$0	$0	$120,000	900	$133

large condo complex, the price is also adjusted for where the condo is located within the building. If the condo is on a higher floor or if it is an end-unit, it will demand more money – people prefer those units over those on the lower floors and in the middle of the complex. Your real estate agent should provide you with this type of information, and any other specific draws or uniqueness of properties that affect the purchase price.

Timing

In general – regardless of the extent of renovations – try not to buy your vacation property at peak season. Both of our Michigan properties rent year round, but winter is the busy season for the Ski Condo. Not surprisingly, winter is also the season many sellers put their condos on the market. Winter sellers typically ask top dollar at peak season. However, sometimes a good deal comes on the market and you just have to act on it, regardless of what time of year it is. This is what happened with our Ski Condo. Your agent should always update you on new market listings, and keep you updated on what is selling in the area. That way, when a good deal comes on the market, you will be able to spot it instantly and act on it immediately.

The Ski Condo rents year-round, so it wasn't a big deal to buy during peak season. Conversely, I looked at condos in Florida that have their peak rental season in January through April, and very little, if any, rentals during the rest of the year. If I had bought a Florida condo in April, I would have had to wait nine months for any rental income. Keep this in mind! If you can afford to go nine months without rental income, then great: go for it! If the price is right, it's possible to buy at any time of the year. I just want you to be aware that your rental income may be seasonal, and you should try to time your purchase as best you can.

Income

At this point you are looking at buying potential vacation homes with your real estate agent, and you must know how to calculate a break-even analysis. You will have to estimate the expenses of buying and renting the home, and how much income you will need to generate each year in order to break even.

What I will explain in the following three sections are: (1) how to determine your projected rental income, (2) what are the basic expenses you will most likely incur, and (3) how to compute the break-even math. This process involves input from your real estate agent, other property owners nearby, and rental property listings on the internet.

Let's start by looking at your projected rental income.

Figure out WHEN. Your task is to determine your peak and off-peak rental seasons. What time of year will people want to rent your vacation property, and why? The Lakefront Chalet would attract people in all seasons; however, it is a major destination for trout, steelhead, and salmon fishermen, which means that our peak time is fishing season. Fishing season takes place in the spring and in the fall. If there is snow on the ground, we can attract snowmobilers in the winter. There are a couple of small ski hills within a half-hour drive, so we might get a weekend rental or two from skiers. But would I get anyone to rent it in the summer? The Lakefront Chalet is in the middle of nowhere. Surprisingly, after a year of advertising, we had our summers fully booked up with weekly rentals! At the Ski Condo, the peak season is late December through the end of March, renting to skiers. Before we purchased the condo, I had many discussions with my real estate agent and other property owners, trying to determine how often the condo would rent during the off-peak season. We discovered that the Ski Condo rented on every major holiday, and during the spring and summer for golfers and summer vacationers. When I looked into buying a condo in Florida, people there told me that the peak season is January through April, and to expect few if any rentals during any other time of the year.

The next step is to figure out the TYPE of rentals you expect to have: by the day, by the weekend, by the week, or by the month. You must decide whether to require a minimum night's stay. For holiday weekends such as Memorial Day, we require renters to book a minimum of three nights. Once you have determined your rental type and the minimum booking, you need to forecast the expected frequency of each rental type. This sounds hard, but don't worry, it is pretty easy to come up with. Your real estate agent should give you a good idea of what types of rentals to expect, and at what times of the year. Don't forget to ask your new neighbors for advice. They have likely been renting their property for many years, and could provide you with a wealth of information. After that, the types of rentals might very well be dictated by the property you have purchased. Many of the Florida condos rented only by the week or by the month, and some didn't allow rentals at all.

At the Ski Condo, peak season skiers rented by the weekend – a short weekend skiing getaway with the family and holiday long-weekends (i.e., Friday through Monday, MLK weekend, Memorial Day weekend, and so on). In the summer the condo rented weekly to summer vacationers. I also anticipated a sporadic mix of week/weekend stays throughout the rest of the year. At the Lakefront Chalet, my family had been vacationing near that property ever since I was a little kid. We had rented many different places in the area, and I had a very good idea of what to expect. I knew from experience that fishermen rented every spring and fall by the week. I anticipated that snowmobilers would rent weekends, and that summer vacation rentals would rent by the week.

See Table 2.2 below for an example of Projected Income.

Table 2.2: Projected Income from Vacation Rental Property

Projected Income	Number of rentals	Rent per Week or Weekend	Total Income per Week or Weekend
Weekly Rentals	5	$2,000	$10,000
Regular Weekend Rentals	10	$1,100	$11,000
Holiday Weekend Rentals	7	$1,700	$11,900
Totals	22		$32,900
Total Yearly Rental Income	$32,900		

The last step is to figure out what to CHARGE. This is easier than you might think. 1) If you have previously vacationed in the area you may already have a good idea what you can charge. Still, make sure to dig deeper and check out your competition. 2) Contact the local Chamber of Commerce, which usually has a website with a link for "lodging." 3) Perform a search on the internet (i.e., using Google) for a brief description of your property, and see what comes up. For example, if you Google "Fort Myers ocean view condo for rent" you will get a plethora of links to many different websites advertising properties similar to yours. 4) Check out the big online advertising sites such as FlipKey, HomeAway, and VRBO to determine what properties like yours are charging. 5) Check out state government sites (i.e., Michigan.org).

Make sure to look at all the amenities and compare apples to apples, because you must get a firm and realistic view of what to charge. There are a lot of condos around our Ski Condo, but ours is unique because it is right on the ski slope, and the ski lift is right outside our back door. Many other condos in our community are not right on the ski run. The Ski Condo has five bedrooms and five bathrooms, whereas most of the other condos have three or four bedrooms with only three or four bathrooms. I determined that I could charge at least as much as a four bedroom condo off the slope. That is what I used to calculate the property's income. During the first year renting the condo we charged just a little bit more than the four bedroom condos off the slopes, and we booked up quickly. The next year we raised our rates to be in line with the advantages our condo had over the others.

When determining what to charge, don't forget to have different sets of rates for different "seasons" (peak/off-peak). You should charge higher rates for holidays and special events. Holidays are any weekends that people get off work. This includes Memorial Day weekend, the fourth of July, Labor Day, Thanksgiving, Christmas, and New Years Eve. Don't forget about Presidents Day (Washington's Birthday), Martin Luther King Day, Good Friday, and any other times you think you can charge more money.

You should also charge more for local special events in the area. At our Ski Condo, the ski hill has special weekends such as "Skitoberfest," "Brew-Ski Festival," and "Krazy Daze." These events bring thousands of renters to the ski mountain, and every condo owner charges higher rates for these special weekends. We also require a minimum three-nights stay on many of the holiday weekends.

If you use GetawayX.com to build your own website, you will be able to easily enter your rates, and any special holiday overrides for specific dates.

See the sample "Rates and Dates" table below (Table 2.3).

Table 2.3: Rates and Dates

Dates[1]	**Nightly** Weeknight/ Holiday	**Weekend[2]** Nightly	**Weekly**	**Monthly**
Summer, Spring and Fall **Apr 1, 2014 - Nov 30, 2014** 2 night minimum stay	$210.00	$450.00	$1,900.00	—
Memorial Day Weekend **May 23, 2014 - May 26, 2014[3]** 3 night minimum stay	$650.00	—	—	—
4th of July **Jul 4, 2014 - Jul 6, 2014[3]** 2 night minimum stay	$650.00	—	—	—
Labor Day Weekend **Aug 29, 2014 - Sep 1, 2014[3]** 3 night minimum stay	$650.00	—	—	—
Winter Ski Season 2014/2015 **Dec 1, 2014 - Mar 31, 2015** 2 night minimum stay	$290.00	$590.00	$2,450.00	—

[1] A one-time cleaning fee of $100 applies to all rentals. Rates change, please call to verify the rate.

[2] Weekends are Friday and Saturday night stays. The rate is for each individual night.

[3] Holiday Rate.

It's also a great idea to call rental management companies in the area and ask them a ton of questions. Tell them that you might be buying a property in the area and renting it to vacationers. Ask them for the peak and off-peak times, the going rates, when potential renters call them, what amenities do renters want in a property, and the standards for renting. Are weekly rentals typically Saturday to Saturday or Sunday through Sunday? I have always set our weekly rentals Sunday to Sunday, because I can then fit in a weekend rental Friday to Sunday. That isn't possible renting Saturday to Saturday.

Learn the rental policies of the other property owners and at least match what they offer so that you are competitive with them.

Do not charge too much or too little – both are big mistakes. When I bought my first vacation rental property, I was afraid that I might not be able to rent it, and priced it really low versus my competition. When inquiries came in, some people asked us what was wrong with the property. Moreover, charging low rent attracted undesirable renters.

If you charge too little, you run the risk that people will think your property isn't as nice as the others. On the other hand, if you charge too much, they will expect more from you than your competition is offering. The best bet is to charge in line with your competition.

Always take a step back and ask yourself: if you were a vacationer looking to rent a property, what would you pay to rent your property?

The final consideration is whether to charge a cleaning fee to your renters. Realistically, it's not up to you to decide. I strongly recommend that you follow what other vacation rentals like yours in the area are doing. If a lot of them charge a cleaning fee, then you should too. But if nobody (or only a few) in the area charge this fee, don't.

While researching rates for our Ski Condo, I noticed that most owners charged a cleaning fee, so I charge a comparable cleaning fee. No renter has ever questioned it. A cleaning fee in the Lakefront Chalet area is unheard of, however, and I don't charge a cleaning fee at that property.

Expenses

Now that we have gone over the projection of rental income, the next step is to get a grasp on your property's estimated expenses. The main expenses your property will incur are: 1) mortgage payment, 2) property taxes, 3) property insurance, 4) utilities, 5) advertising, 6) cleaning, and 7) maintenance. As with all income projections, make realistic assumptions on your expenses.

Many of these expense numbers can be determined by talking to other property owners, your lender, and your real estate agent. Your real estate agent can ask the seller what the utility bills were for the past year, and in addition, provide you with a good estimate of your property taxes. Other property owners and your real estate agent could provide you with referrals to cleaning persons, or simply ask a neighbor what they pay for cleaning. Your mortgage broker, or any online mortgage calculator, can provide you with an estimate of your mortgage payment.

It is recommended that you contact your insurance agent for an estimate of your yearly insurance costs, which can vary greatly depending on where you are buying. For example, you may be required to pay more for special hurricane and flood insurance in parts of Florida, but not so much on a ski hill in Northern Michigan. Advertising costs will vary depending on what forms of advertising you employ. My estimate for advertising below is a good start. Remember that from time to time you will also incur yearly maintenance costs. The "Maintenance" expense (see Table 2.4) is an estimate of what I expect to spend each year in miscellaneous fix-ups and annual maintenance performed on one of my properties. Please note that you may not be able to get an exact number for all the expenses mentioned above. Your goal here is to get very realistic estimates.

Your expenses may also include a Homeowner Association Fee (HOA), sometimes called "Association Dues" or "Condo Dues." These fees can vary greatly, ranging from $50 per month for small condo in the Detroit suburbs to $1500 per month for condos on Lakeshore Drive in Chicago. If you are buying a condo, you must know what services are provided by the HOA dues. As an example, these HOA dues could include cable TV, landscaping, snow removal, insurance on the building (not the inside of the condo unit or your belongings), utilities (water, gas, electric), common area maintenance, or even a doorman. This helps you when computing your break-even analysis.

Table 2.4: Estimated Expenses for Vacation Rental property

Projected Expenses	Monthly	Annual
Mortgage[1]	$1,085	$13,020
Monthly HOA/Condo Dues	$400	$4,800
Property Taxes	$450	$5,400
Cleaning[2]	$238	$2,856
Electric (Utility)	$100	$1,200
Gas (Utility)	$300	$3,600
Water (Utility)[3]	$0	$0
Property Insurance	$80	$960
Cable/Satellite TV (Utility)[4]	$0	$0
Advertising[5]	$100	$1,200
Maintenance	$200	$2,400
Trash Removal (Utility)[6]	$0	$0
Snow removal/yard maintenance[7]	$0	$0
Total Expenses	$2,953	$35,436

[1] Mortgage is financing $214,000 at 4.5% for 30 years

[2] Cleaning is based on number of projected rentals. In this case the property will rent 22 times a year and the cost is $130 for each cleaning

[3] Water is included in the Condo Dues

[4] Cable/Satellite TV is included in the Condo Dues

[5] Advertising expense is based on spending $1200 per year

[6] Trash removal is included in the Condo Dues

[7] Snow removal/yard maintenance is included in the Condo Dues

If you are buying a condo that has an association, you must also inspect the condo association documents and the association reserves. The reserve represents cash on hand to fix and upgrade the building. If the reserve is low and the building needs an update or something replaced, chances are the association will create a "Special Assessment," and bill each condo unit accordingly to cover the cost. It's a good idea to make sure there are no pending special assessments, or any ongoing issues. You could be financially responsible for them after purchasing the property!

The best way to find out what's really going on at a condominium complex is to 1) ask other property owners for their opinion on the Association, and 2) have your real estate agent get a copy of the association meeting minutes and their financials for the past few years.

Reading the Association's meeting minutes can be eye-opening. Sometimes you will find a lot of information on what is going well, and not well, within the community. When buying a condo, please make sure to solicit the advice of your real estate agent.

Break Even Analysis

Now that you have a good idea of what income and expenses to expect, the last step is to do the math and figure out your break-even point.

Breaking even simply means that your total yearly income equals or exceeds your total yearly expenses. Your goal here might be to come close to break-even, to break-even, or to have a positive cash flow over your expenses.

Be realistic with your analysis of the math, and if you have to lean one way, make sure to underestimate your income and overestimate your expenses. In one morning of previewing potential properties you can easily perform a break-even analysis.

Table 2.2 and Table 2.4 above are the projected Income and Expenses charts I calculated prior to purchasing our Ski Condo. I estimated conservatively because, most likely, you will not completely book your property the first year you own it. It does take some time to get the word out and to get your property on the rental scene. During the first year we brought in more income than projected, but not enough to totally cover the yearly expenses. This was completely okay with us because the Ski Condo is a vacation home, and we used it ourselves over those twelve months. The mortgage and most of the costs associated with the property were paid by our renters. If we had bought the property only for a vacation home, we would have had these expenses anyway. In year two, you should expect more rentals and income because you will have repeat renters.

The income and expense projections for a property not on the lake near our Lakefront Chalet are summarized below in Tables 2.5 and 2.6.

The sample income and expenses tables above should help you to determine if the math works for you or not. Again, it is up to you whether you want to break even. Some people may be okay not generating a profit, and others may only want to own a vacation property to generate positive cash flow. I recommend that you do the math prior to making an offer on any property so that you have an idea what you are getting yourself into.

Other Revenue

Over the years I looked for ways to make money with my vacation rental properties other than through rental income. Recently, I created an online store through Zazzle.com to sell coffee mugs and t-shirts with our property name/logo and website on them. It was extremely easy to do, and it is integrated into my property's website on GetawayX.com.

Table 2.5: Projected Income (non-lake property near the Lakefront Chalet)

Projected Income	Number of rentals	Amount of Rent per Week or Weekend	Total Income per Week or Weekend
Summer Weekly Rentals	7	$1,195	$8,365
Fall and Spring Weekly Rentals	7	$1,195	$8,365
Regular Weekend Rentals	6	$395	$2,370
Holiday Weekend Rentals	6	$550	$3,300
Totals	26		$22,400
Total Yearly Rental Income	$22,400		

You have the ability to do the same thing on your GetawayX website. Not only does this generate a little extra income every year, it creates "stickiness." Stickiness is making your renters "stick" with you and keep renting from you. If a renter buys a coffee mug with your property name on it, and uses it every day, who do you think they will call for their next vacation rental? You, of course! It is also an awesome advertising tool. If your renter takes the coffee mug to work, their co-workers (your target market) will ask about that coffee mug, which will start a conversation on how awesome your place is.

Another way to generate additional income is with online advertising. You have the option to put your own Google AdSense advertising on your GetawayX website and generate advertising revenue. In order to do this, sign up with Google and get an AdSense account. After that, you can easily add the advertising to your property's website in the Command Center at GetawayX.com.

Table 2.6: Projected Expenses (non-lake property near the Lakefront Chalet)

Projected Expenses	Monthly	Annual
Mortgage[1]	$429	$5,148
Monthly HOA/Condo Dues	$0	$0
Property Taxes	$167	$2,000
Cleaning[2]	$174	$2,080
Electric	$50	$600
Gas	$100	$1,200
Water[3]	$0	$0
Property Insurance	$60	$720
Cable/Satellite TV	$55	$660
Advertising[4]	$100	$1,200
Maintenance	$150	$1,800
Trash Removal	$40	$480
Snow removal/yard maintenance	$50	$600
Total Expenses	$1,375	$16,500

[1]Mortgage is financing $80,000 at 5% for 30 years

[2]Cleaning is based on number of projected rentals. We will rent the property 26 times a year and the cost is $80 for each cleaning

[3]Water is free (well water)

[4]Advertising expense is based on spending $1200 per year

The final revenue generating idea is to provide links to local attractions, restaurants, or bars on your website. Contact local restaurants, bars, and any business that might want to advertise on your site. You then charge them an agreed upon fee. Why would a local business advertise on your site? Because prospective renters who come to your site are locked-in target market clients for local advertisers. You can also offer your advertisers an opportunity to place a welcome kit with coupons in your rental property.

Make an Offer and Negotiate

At this point you have found a desirable property that is legally feasible for you to rent, and you are comfortable with the projected math. Now you should put in an offer on the property you like best. We made offers on many ski condos before we had an acceptance. Every offer I made was based on the math, and on the fair market value of the property. It is always good if you can get a good deal on a property, but when investing this way, you really just need the math to work for you. Here's an example.

Let's say that condos not directly on the ski slope go for $300,000, and you have the chance to buy one for $285,000. Sounds awesome, right? Yes, you are buying it for $15,000 less than fair market value, but remember your math. Based on a 30-year mortgage at 5%, that $15,000 is only $80 less per month on your mortgage payment, and hardly budges your break-even math. The same goes for paying more. Let's say that ski-in ski-out condos directly on the ski slopes go for $330,000. That $30,000 extra you are paying to have the DRAW of being on the ski slope costs $162 more per month (about $2,000 more per year). That sounds like a lot of money, but the added draw of walking out the back door directly onto the chairlift demands more rent than condos not on the slope (location, location, location). I rent twelve ski weekends and charge an extra $200 for being right on the hill; which is $2,400 more in rent. That $2,400 easily covers the extra $2,000 in mortgage payments each year. Remember that people vacationing want a draw!

And don't forget to ask yourself what *you* would like. This property is being purchased for the long run, and you will be using it as well.

When the time comes to make an offer on a property, you will have seen many properties, either in person with your agent, or via your own research on the internet. You will have a good idea of what properties in the area are going for, and what you should pay. Come up with a figure that is the MOST you would pay for the property, and make it your agent's goal to get the property at a price lower than that. You should also ask your real estate agent to look over your projected income and expenses, and get the agent's opinion on whether your estimates are realistic.

Next, discuss contingencies with your agent, and other items he or she recommends to be included in the Purchase Agreement. A contingency is something you put in your purchase agreement that makes the deal "contingent" upon something. It gives you a way out of the deal.

I would recommend a few basic contingencies: 1) a satisfactory inspection of the property, 2) time to determine if the property can be rented as a vacation home, and 3) if the property is a condo, a satisfactory review of all HOA documents and meeting notes. Get advice from a professional real estate agent, because there may be more contingencies your agent can recommend, depending on the area in which you are buying. A termite inspection, for example, which is not that common here in Michigan, but might be more standard in the South.

Most vacation properties will be sold with all of its furniture, linens, and pots and pans: almost everything in there will be included. In other words, the sale should be turn-key. If the property is not ready-to-rent, add this into your upfront costs. A purchase offer for real estate is just that: to purchase the real estate. The other items inside the property are considered personal property. Your agent may recommend a separate "bill of sale" for all of the personal property in the transaction.

Once you have a grasp on the maximum price, contingencies, what is included in the property, and your upfront fix-up costs, you are ready to make an offer. Your agent will provide you with advice on an initial offer price, and negotiating techniques. Sometimes it is best to offer the seller a fair price and say, "take it or leave it." At other times it's appropriate to play the game of offering a low price in the beginning and negotiating back and forth, eventually coming close to the maximum you want to pay for the property. I have used the technique of adding several more contingencies or additional items to the purchase agreement, and then, when countering the seller, I would take a few of these off. This demonstrates to the seller that I am not only willing to come up in price, but to also drop some of my additional conditions (contingencies that I really didn't care about in the first place.)

In summary: first and foremost you want to buy in an area where you like to vacation, and would enjoy in your retirement. Once you zero in on an area, get a good real estate agent and determine what you can afford, the rental feasibility, and the break-even math. From there, it is a matter of negotiating and closing the deal!

Chapter Recap

- You must determine the DRAW of the property/area you are buying.

- Not all vacation homes need be expensive.

- A good, attentive, experienced real estate agent should be part of your team as your "buyer's agent." You should tell your agent what you are trying to achieve.

- Before purchasing a property, find out if there are rental restrictions.

- When looking at potential properties, keep a list of the fix-up costs and repairs/upgrades necessary for a 'comparable' property to your competition.
- Figure out the "When," "Type," and "Charge" for your rental income.
- Do the math, compare properties, and make an offer.

Chapter 3

Inspection

What you will learn . . .

- How the inspection process works
- How to choose a property inspector

. . . and more!

I am not a property inspector. However, I have learned a lot of tips over the years from buying real estate, and through my research. At first glance, the property you are looking at may appear not to need any repairs. But there may be problems hiding in areas where you are not looking. For example, inspections often discover mold in the attic or basement, or other areas hidden from view.

Most forms of mold are not dangerous, but remediating the mold and fixing the problem that caused the mold can cost you thousands of dollars. This is why it is important to hire a professional property inspector to inspect the property before you buy it.

Even if the property is a brand new home, a bank owned property, or sold "as-is," I strongly recommend that you have the property inspected prior to your purchase. The goal of this chapter is to give you a basic knowledge of the inspection process, and how to choose an inspector.

The Inspection Process

When you make an offer on a property, include a condition in the contract that the offer is contingent upon a satisfactory property inspection. This doesn't mean that you are relying on an FHA, VA, or City inspection that might be required to purchase the property. Rather, you want to hire a professional property inspector or company to perform a complete inspection of the property. You and your real estate agent will determine how long you will have to complete the inspection (i.e., within seven days of a signed offer), and the terms when reporting the findings back to the seller. If nothing substantial is found, the inspection contingency will be lifted from the contract and the transaction will continue to closing.

If there are significant issues discovered in the inspection process, you, the buyer, will typically 1) walk away from the deal, 2) ask the seller to fix the issues, or 3) ask the seller to pay you to get them fixed, normally in the form of reducing the contract price. If you choose to have the seller perform the repairs, consult with your real estate agent and have a new condition added to the contract; a condition that says you have the option to re-inspect the property after the repairs are completed. You want your inspector re-inspect what the seller did to fix the problems, because you do not want to take the seller's word that the repairs were done satisfactorily, or even completed at all. If permits were needed to do the work, get copies of them and the results of the permit's inspections. In other words, make sure that the work was completed to your satisfaction. If it wasn't completed to your satisfaction, you should have in your contract the option to once again walk away from the deal, or to have the seller pay you to fix the property to your satisfaction.

I realize that you may be buying a property that is far away from your home, but if at all possible, I recommend that you walk around with the inspector while they are doing the inspection, and look at everything he/she is looking at. Ask as many questions as you can think of, and take notes. A property inspection can be an eye-opening experience if you have never participated in one. If you have maintenance questions about appliances and equipment at the property, ask the inspector. A good inspector will be a fountain of knowledge!

After the inspection has been completed, you should be provided with a very detailed report, along with suggestions for yearly maintenance. A typical property inspection report will be about 25–70 pages long, depending on what is found. The report will have sections, broken down by the property's exterior and interior, with a lot of pictures and comments, including the weather conditions on the day of the inspection. The exterior section should include comments on the condition of the garage, roof, chimney, siding, windows, foundation, and drainage. The interior sections should include comments about the condition of the attic, ventilation, electrical system, plumbing, heating and cooling systems, water heater, fireplace, flooring, smoke and carbon monoxide detectors, walls, appliances (dishwasher, range, stove, refrigerator), water flow in bathrooms, basement (structure, water damage, dampness, etc.), and the results of radon testing. The report should summarize the overall inspection results, outlining specific major concerns and major safety concerns, as well as providing you with items you should repair, items to monitor, and items to maintain.

The Property Inspector

A lot of people call themselves property inspectors. The inspector you hire is the last person to look at your property for problems, so you must not casually select your inspector. Don't hire any random inspector that is referred to you; rather, I recommend that you perform your due diligence.

You will find that there are full-time and part-time inspectors. Full-time inspectors perform about 400 property inspections per year. Part-time inspectors may claim to have been in business for over a decade, but often these guys complete fewer than 200 inspections per year. I recommend that you hire a full-time inspector who will work in your best interest. An inspector who performs more inspections, especially on properties similar to the one you are buying, is more valuable because a more experienced inspector will be able to better point out potential issues. How many years they have been in business is less important than how many inspections they perform per year, primarily on properties like the one you are buying. If you are buying a condo and a potential inspector only has experience with single-family homes, he might not be your best choice. You want an inspector familiar with the type of property you are buying, and who has experience inspecting that type of property.

Question all potential inspectors or inspection companies. Your goal is to find an inspector who has attended a professional school, is a member of a national organization, has passed a criminal background check, and who is fully insured and bonded.

Many states, such as Michigan, do not require licensed property inspectors, and they are not regulated by the state. What this means is that anyone can make up some business cards and call himself a property inspector. Therefore, once you have gotten a few referrals, ask the inspector these questions:

- Are they professionally trained and if so, what company do they work for and what certifications do they hold? It is recommended that your inspector be a member of the National Association of Home Inspectors (NAHI) or the American Society of Home Inspectors (ASHI). These are the two big national groups for property inspectors. In addition, if your property has a septic system or a well, ensure that the inspector is a certified well and septic inspector.

- Find out if the inspector has passed the National Home Inspectors Exam (NHIE). In states that license inspectors, individuals must pass this exam before being allowed to conduct business. Even if your state doesn't license inspectors, many of them will take the test anyway, and put it on their resume for added credibility.

- Next, ask questions about insurance, specifically regarding Errors & Omissions (E&O), Worker's Compensation (Workman's Comp), and General Liability insurance. If your inspector screws up or misses a major problem at the property, E&O insurance is there for you. If your inspector falls off the roof during the inspection and is injured, do they have Workman's Comp to pay for their lost wages? If not, you could be on the hook. If the inspector does something while at the property that creates a problem or damage, who pays? This is where General Liability insurance comes in. Make sure your inspector is insured in all three areas, and request a copy of all their insurance documents.

- This may seem a bit weird, but you should ask if a criminal background check has been performed on the inspector. Remember, in a lot of states, inspectors are not licensed or regulated, so what's going to happen if something comes up missing at the property after the inspection? Moreover, make sure that your inspector is bonded, and request proof.
- Finally, check the Better Business Bureau in the area where the property is located to further evaluate the inspector's credibility.

Once you have a few inspectors to choose from, please do not let price dictate your decision. You should go with the most qualified person, not the cheapest. Your goal is to hire a professional inspector who will work in your best interest, and who is fully trained, experienced, insured, and bonded.

Chapter Recap

- Have the property inspected by a qualified property inspector or company prior to closing.
- A full-time inspector will perform about 400 inspections per year.
- Ask potential inspectors:
  - How many inspections do they perform per year?
  - Are they licensed, and are they professionally trained and certified?
  - Do they have the three types of insurances discussed?
- Double check with the Better Business Bureau.

Chapter 4

Financing

By Sandy Gaulin, Senior Loan Officer

What you will learn . . .

- The types of funding available
- The process of getting a loan

. . . and more!

Now that you have made the decision to purchase an investment property, you will probably need a mortgage, or financing. I would like to spend some time explaining the lending process. Lending and underwriting are all about the evaluation of risk, and establishing the probability that the lender will be repaid.

Mortgagors consider residential, non-owner occupied (income or investment) homes to be the highest risk, and will therefore require a larger investment on the part of the purchaser, and more restrictive underwriting standards, to mitigate that risk. There are essentially four potential sources of funding available in the holiday or vacation rental market: conforming loans, non-conforming loans, portfolio lending, and land contracts.

Types of Funding

Conforming Loans

Briefly, conforming loans are those that fall under the guidelines and guarantees of FNMA (the Federal National Mortgage Association, aka "Fannie Mae") or FHLMC (Federal Home Loan Mortgage Corp., aka "Freddie Mac"). The lending criteria are relatively conservative and must fit within the guidelines of these Government Sponsored Entities (GSEs). Conforming loans are readily available and typically come with competitive rates and fees. However, conforming loans include limitations on loan size and property type, as well as conservative approaches to underwriting.

Non-conforming Loans

Non-conforming loans are often offered by the same lenders as conforming products, but are backed by private investors and not GSEs. Consequently, non-conforming loans have more leeway with regard to underwriting practices and interpretations. These loans are typically less restrictive on property type, have higher loan limits, and may have fewer documentation requirements for certain borrowers. That being said, the trade-off for fewer restrictions can mean higher rates and fees, or limitations on loan products such as Adjustable Rate Mortgage (ARM) loans versus Fixed Rate Loans.

Portfolio Lending

The third type of typically available financing is portfolio lending. Quite often, these loans are provided by a local or private bank, or the bank that is funding the project that includes the property you are buying. Portfolio lending is common for "CondoTel" type properties, or in developments where the property type and occupancy do not meet conforming guidelines. (In a Condotel property, investors own individual condo units and an on-site rental management program operates each unit like a hotel room.) Portfolio lending may also be available to borrowers who have income or employment that does not meet the requirements of conforming lenders.

Land Contracts

Land contracts are another form of financing that may be available to an individual purchasing a vacation/income property. Land contracts can easily be defined as "seller financing" because the purchaser will essentially borrow from and make their payments directly to the current property owner (seller). Land contracts are very useful in cases where your credit, your income, your assets, the property type, occupancy constraints, or circumstances do not allow the purchaser to obtain financing through typical channels. A land contract allows the purchaser to buy the property and take possession of it; however, they do not take title to the property until the contract is paid off. Land contracts are typically "balloon" style loans, which means that within a few years of the initial purchase, the new owner must pay off the seller, or risk defaulting on the contract and returning ownership to the seller. Typically, under a balloon payment, the buyer obtains alternative financing to pay off the seller.

Getting a Loan

With the exception of the land contract, the process for getting a loan is similar: application, processing, underwriting, and closing.

Application

The application process is where everything starts. Typically, the prospective home buyer will meet with a lender/loan officer and complete an application. The physical application will be the guiding document for the transaction and will basically be a written description of your income, assets, and credit, a brief history of your work and residency, and a summary of the transaction. The application will include several disclosures and attestations, many specific to the governing state and federal laws for real estate transactions. Where the process becomes complicated, and where most borrowers become most frustrated with the application process, is in documenting all of the information that is listed and described in the application itself. This is when it is best to keep two things in mind: 1) remember that "lending is all about risk and evaluating that risk to insure repayment," and 2) financing for the home is not a loan against the property; it is a loan against your income (your ability to repay). The property itself is only the collateral for the loan.

> Verifying and documenting income can be one of the most trying steps in the process of underwriting a mortgage application, especially for self-employed borrowers. Be prepared to provide a lot of documentation. When evaluating income, the lender is looking for stability and sustainability.

Because the best way to predict the future is to evaluate history, the lender is going to ask you for (at minimum) a two-year history of earnings. This means your personal and/or business returns, W2s, and 1099s for the last two full calendar years, as well as year-to-date earnings for the current year. When the lender asks for these items, they will ask you to provide "All pages and schedules," and they mean it. Every document filed with your return should be sent to the lender, and if anything is missing, the processing of your loan application will likely be stopped until you provide it.

The lender will inspect every reported source of your income and potential loss. Considering that most people now file their returns electronically, it is usually not a problem for a borrower (or their accountant) to simply pull a file from their computer and send it off to the lender as part of the application support documentation. But if you still file a hard copy return, make sure that all pages are sent to the lender to avoid delays. Make sure that you send all information from your tax returns to the lender, because the lender will request a copy of your returns from the IRS (aka "the 4506"), and will compare the information on your physical return to the information on the transcript, to insure that the information you reported to the IRS matches what was given to the lender.

> One last thing about income: If you don't report it to the IRS, it doesn't exist.

After income, the most important component of the loan application is your assets. Assets are defined as liquid funds, vested funds, and real estate owned (cash in the bank, investments, retirement plan investments, and property owned.) Using this information, the lender is going to document three things: (1) your funds to close, (2) money for reserves, and (3) the source of funds you intend to use to purchase the property. Keep in mind that when purchasing an investment property using conventional, non-conforming, or portfolio lending financing, the lender will require a minimum down payment (or investment) of 20% of the purchase price, and often that number can be 25%.

In addition to the down payment, the buyer must pay closing and other transaction costs. On a $200,000 transaction, these other costs could be 1% to 10% of the property price. The lender will obviously confirm that you actually have the money to satisfy the transaction, as well as documenting the source of those funds. Additionally, it is now commonplace to require a borrower with multiple properties to have reserves sufficient to make the principal, interest, taxes, insurance, and/or association dues payments on all your properties for a minimum of six months. Therefore, if you have three properties, (a primary home, a second home, and an investment) that each have a $1,000 monthly obligation, you will need to document an additional $18,000 in assets over and above what is needed for the transaction.

When documenting funds, the lender is going to ask for a minimum of the last two months' full bank statements for any "liquid" accounts – checking, savings, money market, CD, or anything that you can get at your bank and/or credit union and that can be accessed immediately. You will also be asked to provide the most recent statement for any stock, bond, mutual fund, IRA, 401K, annuity, or investment accounts used to draw funds for the transaction, or which you use for reserves. If you are drawing funds from this type of account, you will be required to provide terms and conditions of withdrawal for the account.

For example, many retirement accounts allow the account holder to borrow funds against the vested balance, but in doing so there is now a repayment schedule associated with that loan. The lender will need to know those terms. (Please note: you must confirm that your 401K plan allows funds to be drawn for real estate transactions, and particularly the purchase of second and/or investment properties.)

When the lender asks for the statements or documentation for these accounts, the request is for ALL PAGES.

If your bank statement says the statement is six pages long and the sixth page is completely blank, provide it nonetheless. If your investment account statement is 146 pages and 144 of those document minor stock swaps or rebalancing, you will still need to provide all pages. Not doing so will stop the application in its tracks.

Why does the lender request all pages? The first and simplest answer is documenting the sources of funds. The lender is tasked with insuring that all monies in the transaction are the borrower's own funds, and to do that they will look at any deposit into the accounts during the last sixty days that are unusual or large, and which are not electronic/direct deposits or transfers between the applicant's own accounts. Monies received from outside sources are potential areas of risk. If an applicant has borrowed funds from another individual or institution, the repayment of that loan may affect their ability to repay the subject loan.

Be prepared to document that all of the funds required for the transaction are yours, and that you can provide a paper trail for the source of those funds.

The third main component is credit history and credit scoring. A credit score is simply a mathematical interpretation of a borrower's willingness and ability to repay consumer debt. The most common scoring model for mortgage loans is the Fair Isaac Score (FICO), which has a range between 350 and 850. The higher the score, the better is the credit history and therefore, the lower risk to the lender. In a mortgage transaction, a lender will pull what is known as a "Tri-Merge" credit report, which collects data from the three major credit reporting bureaus (Equifax, TransUnion, and Experion). The tri-merge report ensures that the lender is receiving the most complete and accurate data regarding a borrower's credit history.

Depending on the circumstances of your history, you may be asked to document and explain any of the following: divorce, bankruptcy, foreclosure, deed-in-lieu, business losses, multiple property ownership, new or recent credit inquiries, or any other data found in your credit or public record that could have an effect on your ability to qualify for a loan. These items are normally addressed in the processing and underwriting of the loan.

Processing

Loan processing is the task of gathering and organizing all pertinent data required by an underwriter to make a decision on a loan. A loan processor will verify all of the information provided in an application: employment and job histories, income, assets, title and lien histories on the property, appraisals, and so on. The processor collects all of this data and packages it for submission to an underwriter, where a loan decision will be made.

Underwriting

Underwriters have the unenviable task of considering all of the data in a loan file, and determining whether the loan fits the guidelines of the product and investors, whether the borrower has demonstrated the ability and willingness to repay the debt and has sufficient assets and reserves, determining that the property meets the requirements for the purpose of the loan, and that sufficient collateral exists. Assuming that the file meets all the requirements, it is approved and will be closed and funded.

Closing

Following the approval of the lender, a closing is scheduled. Normally performed by a Title Insurance Agency, a closing is where the real estate and mortgage transactions are completed. All legal documents for the mortgage and the property transfer are executed and witnessed, and the deeds and mortgages are then sent to be recorded in the public record.

Borrowing and Real Estate as an Investment

The common theme here is an evaluation of the prospective borrower, defined as the individual(s) purchasing the property. Mortgage banks, and the mortgage products described here, are for persons, not businesses. While it is common for individuals who purchase investment property to put them into LLCs following the transaction, it is recommended that you read and understand the mortgage and any potential "due on sale" or "due on transfer" clauses or restrictions on deed transfers. Each state typically has its own mortgage language. Because the laws vary from state to state, it may be prudent to consult with a real estate attorney in your jurisdiction, to insure that when transferring the property deed into an LLC, you do not jeopardize your financing.

> Whether the property is held as an individual or in an LLC, it IS a business. Therefore, how much you borrow, what type of loan you use, and how you structure it are all part of the cash-flow on it. The monthly payment, including taxes, insurance, and any association dues, is the lion's share of the monthly budget and affects your profitability.

When making a decision on a vacation rental property, you will ideally know the rental rates for that property. Based on your profitability goals, this sets your budget for monthly expenditures. By evaluating that budget, the loan officer can assist you to structure a loan that will meet your needs. The question is, how much are you planning to borrow? A minimum investment of 20% is typically required. Do you need to put in more to make the numbers come out where you want, or do you want to only put in the minimum required?

Let's look at a couple of quick examples. Borrowing $200,000 on a 30-year Fixed Rate loan at 6% yields a payment of $1,199.10 per month. Borrowing an additional $20,000 ($220,000) on the same terms would give you a payment of $1,319.01, an increase of approximately $120 a month. The questions of course are, how does this affect your profitability? Do you have or want to invest an additional $20,000 into the transaction? In other words, how much more property do you get for that additional $20,000, and is it a property you can rent at a higher fee to easily cover the extra $120 each month? In short, once you know how much you want to borrow, the question becomes, what are the repayment terms (the terms of the mortgage)?

You will need to decide if you want a Fixed or Adjustable Rate (ARM) mortgage. Fixed loans are stable, and your payment is fixed to a specific payment amount per month, giving you long-term security in your monthly cost. ARMs could have more risk, but usually offer a lower initial interest rate, which can possibly lead to better cash flow for you as an investor. (Keep in mind that the ARM option may be the only one available in the "non-conforming" lending arena.) One of the first questions to ask is, "How long do I intend to own this property?"

By all means utilize an ARM loan with a three- or five-year lock period if your project is short-term. A 3/1 (sometimes called a 3/27) ARM loan has a guaranteed rate for the first three years, and then becomes an annually adjusting loan for the balance of its 30-year term – in other words, the interest rate will change every year after the initial three-year period. The five- and seven-year versions of an ARM loan are a bit more stable than the three-year version, yet still offer a rate lower than traditional Fixed Rate loans, and that of course means a lower monthly payment.

If you intend to keep your property long term, or are risk adverse and want rate certainty for the life of the loan, choose the Fixed Rate product and let it run its course. The fixed rate also contains less risk for the lender; therefore, you may find a lower upfront cost and an easier qualifying process. The bottom line is that you should look at each option, Fixed and ARM, long and short amortizations, to see how it fits your goals with the property.

On top of the basic loan structure, consider how to handle taxes and insurance on your vacation rental property. Escrowing – having the annual taxes and insurance collected by the lender on a monthly basis and then paid to the taxing authority or insurer when billed – has some benefits in an investment property scenario. First, it gives you consistent cash flow over the year and avoids the "payment shock" of the tax bill once or twice a year (depending on how tax bills are issued in your city, state, or county). Second, lenders actually charge a fee to waive an escrow account, typically 0.25 of a discount point. This could make a difference of $500.00 in your closing costs on a $200,000 loan, or perhaps 0.125% on the interest rate. While many people prefer not to have the lender holding on to their money throughout the year, escrowing may be considered a benefit in the long-term ownership and management of your property.

Other Items

If you choose not to go with traditional lending to finance your vacation rental properties, it pays to perform your due diligence. As mentioned, a common method used to finance a unique property is a land contract. Because land contracts are a financing agreement between buyer and seller, you will want to ensure that your interests are protected. Be aware of this key piece of information when buying a property using land contract financing: the seller cannot offer a land contract for a property that has a mortgage lien in place; in other words, the seller in a land contract must own the property free and clear with no liens. A title search should be performed to ensure that there are no liens on the property. You will most likely want to have a real estate agent, real estate attorney, and/or Title Company involved to make sure that everything is done and recorded correctly. Sample land contracts can easily be found online, and are a good starting point if you choose to go that route.

Another source of funds is retirement assets. Before you commit to this source of funds, however, be sure to read and understand the terms and conditions of withdrawal of those assets. Most Retirement Savings Accounts only allow funds to be utilized for primary home transactions, not second homes or investment properties. In addition, you may have heard of people converting their 401k or IRA from investing in stocks to buying investment real estate. Yes, this can be done, but it doesn't fit for our method of investing in real estate. You see, if you convert your 401k or IRA to buy investment real estate, you cannot use the property yourself – at all. One of the benefits of buying vacation property as an investment is so that you can enjoy it every year!

I have described to you the types of financing, and the process of obtaining a loan. The minute you decide to look for a property, make sure to contact your mortgage broker. Tell them that you intend to buy a vacation property and rent it. Review your financing options with your mortgage broker as I have described. If both of you agree that you can afford the purchase, get a pre-approval letter from your lender, which simply states that you are "approved" to borrow a certain amount of money to buy a property. Most sellers will ask for a pre-approval letter from the borrower on a purchase agreement, and it is a good idea to have this already completed and ready to provide when asked for.

The main thing to remember is: lending and underwriting is all about the evaluation of risk and establishing the probability that the lender will be repaid.

Chapter Recap

- Lenders consider non-owner occupied investment properties to be high risk.
- Lending standards can be more stringent for investment properties.
- Verifying and documenting income can be one of the most trying steps in the process of underwriting a mortgage application, especially for self-employed borrowers.
- Different types of loans can make your monthly payment higher or lower, which can affect your monthly cash flow, and the time frame for paying off the property.

- Make sure to have an experienced quality mortgage broker on your team!

Chapter 5

Insurance

By John T. Frye, Jr., Managing Partner of Doeren Mayhew Insurance Group

What you will learn . . .

- Different ways insurance can protect you and your investment
- Insurance for rental real estate

. . . and more!

Insurance is an extremely important part of this investment strategy. If the policy you purchase to cover your investment property is not written properly, your investment could quickly be turned upside down.

The good news is that in general, the process of insuring a vacation rental property should be quite simple. However, there are a few key types of coverage to consider when purchasing your policy.

I strongly recommend using an independent agent or agency with access to various carriers and markets that can customize a policy to fit your exact needs. Typically, direct writers of insurance (the big insurance companies), have less flexible and more standardized policies that may not meet your specific coverage needs. Furthermore, independent agents or agencies typically have access to multiple carriers that offer various products, which usually results in more specific coverage. In addition, the creation of competition between carriers results in more value for your dollar.

Dwelling Limit

The first step in securing insurance for your property is providing your agent with an accurate description of the property in order to come up with an accurate dwelling limit. The dwelling limit is the amount of insurance necessary to replace your home in the event of a total loss. If this limit is inaccurate or low, major issues could arise in the event of a large loss.

You must be comfortable with the dwelling coverage limit that your agent includes in his or her proposal. If possible, provide your agent with a copy of the bank's appraisal, because it will provide good detail of the structure you are insuring. As with a standard homeowners' insurance policy, the dwelling limit is typically the starting point of any policy. This will hold true in the case of vacation rental property as well.

Contents Insurance

In most cases you will buy a dwelling fire policy or a non-owner occupied policy, but contents coverage will not be included in the policy as it is with a standard homeowner's policy. Contents insurance is insurance that pays for damage to, or loss of, an individual's personal possessions while they are located within that individual's home. Some contents insurance policies also provide restricted coverage for personal possessions temporarily taken away from the home by the policyholder. It will be necessary for you to provide the agent with a coverage limit for the contents in any property you own. Do not overlook this; imagine a total loss in which none of your furniture or furnishings is covered!

Rent Guarantee Insurance

> It is recommended that rent guarantee insurance be included in any policy you purchase. Rent guarantee is a form of insurance whereby, for a relatively small annual fee, landlords can protect against loss of rent.

In the event of a loss that makes your property non-rentable, rent guarantee insurance can be critical, depending on your financial exposure. You should consider your financial obligations in the event that you cannot rent the property because of damage caused by a covered peril. For example, if the property is not in use for twelve months while being restored, there could be substantial financial impact to the owner. This insurance covers you for the loss of rental income.

Liability Insurance

As a landlord, financial exposure may not be limited to the property you own. Liability policies address the exposure to financial liability from damage caused to others with regard to the insured's property.

More specifically defined, liability insurance is a part of the general insurance system of risk financing, protecting the purchaser (the "insured") from the risks of liabilities imposed by lawsuits and similar claims. It protects the insured in the event he or she is sued for claims that come within the coverage of the insurance policy.

Commonly, the policy you purchase will specifically provide "landlord liability" insurance as part of your policy. You should consider choosing higher limits of landlord liability for two reasons. First, it is typically very cost effective, and second, lawsuits that are addressed by this portion of your policy can get very expensive. If there is a renter in your property, anything can happen. You should be covered for as much as possible, even a child putting a key in an outlet. Depending on the owner's financial situation, I also recommend the purchase of an umbrella policy which will sit over the "landlord liability limit."

Flood Insurance

In 2012, Congress passed a law affecting the cost of flood insurance in areas with flood issues, including states such as Florida, Massachusetts, New York, and New Jersey. If you purchase a vacation property in an area where flood insurance is required, you will probably have to pay a higher premium for flood insurance than the current owner of the property. In many cases, much higher.

There is some talk in Washington of repealing the law, but so far second homes would still be affected. I have been told that premiums can go up by 25 percent a year until reaching a level consistent with the risk of flooding. This can have a huge impact on costs associated with your property. Talk with your real estate agent and insurance agent to get a firm understanding of your cost for flood insurance.

If you are purchasing a vacation property in a flood zone, or where flood insurance is required, make sure to fully understand the insurance costs BEFORE you make an offer on a property.

Other Forms of Insurance

Depending on where you are buying your property, there may be other forms of insurance you may want to obtain, or be required to obtain. In Florida, due to the nature of hurricanes and tropical storms, you may need to have hurricane, flood, and/or wind insurance. While you are previewing potential properties, ask your real estate agent about specific or special insurance that might be required or recommended. Pose these questions to your insurance agent as well, because special insurance could be costly, and negatively affect your break-even analysis.

Conclusion

There are four main types of coverage to keep in mind when purchasing an insurance policy for your vacation rental policy: dwelling, contents, rent guarantee, and landlord liability. Also consider the quality of the insurance carrier. When a claim goes sideways you must have a quality carrier and strong representation from your agent, otherwise you may be in for a challenging experience. Good luck, and remember to protect your investment!

Chapter Recap

- Your insurance agent must know how to insure vacation rental investment property.

- The insurance you will need is not your typical homeowner's policy.
- Rent Guarantee insurance can protect against loss of rents.
- Landlord Liability with high limits should be considered.
- The quality of the insurance carrier matters.
- Beware if buying in a flood zone – make sure to double check what your insurance rates will be before making an offer.

Chapter 6

Legal

By Jonathan Eadie, Esq., Attorney at Law

What you will learn . . .

- Different ways to protect you and your investment
- How to set up your business
- Are there restrictions in your area?
- Rental agreements and security deposits

. . . and more!

There is an old saying: expect the best, but plan for the worst. This thinking underlines much of the legal profession. Operating a vacation rental property is a business, and you should treat it as such. There are legal obligations you must be aware of, and legal protections available to shield you and your family from harm. This intent of this chapter is to inform you of the potential legal issues you may encounter in establishing and operating your vacation rental property.

Legal Protection for Your Investment

Immediately after you decide to buy a property you must make your first legal decision: who will own and operate the property? Will you own it in your own name, or will you own it in partnership with another person or persons? In most cases the wisest decision, for legal purposes, is to start a new company and operate the property as a separate business.

> If you purchase and operate the property in your own name, or with a partner, you are personally liable not only for the property's bills (such as property taxes, license fees, insurance payments, and special assessments), but also any potential liability created on the property, including the injury of one of your renters.

Personal liability means that all of your personal assets, including your home, your bank accounts, your car, and other property, could be at risk. Suppose a renter falls down the stairs and is seriously injured. If you are inadequately insured, that renter could sue you, and if successful, could take your rental and your personal assets. That is why in almost all cases it is in your best interest to create and operate your vacation rental as a business entity.

LLC and Limited Partnership

In order to encourage small businesses, a hybrid corporate entity has developed over the years: a limited liability company or corporation

(LLC), depending on the state. The LLC allows shareholders or "members" protection from liability without double taxation. The profits of the LLC flow directly to the members without being taxed at the company level. Thus the LLC is taxed like a partnership, but maintains the liability protection of a corporation.

A Limited Partnership (LP) is another corporate hybrid. Generally, a limited partnership will allow for "pass through" of profits while providing a type of protection for the "limited partners." In an LP, one or more partners (the managing partners) operate the business, and remain personally liable for the debts and obligations of the company. The other partners – those with no role in the management of the company – are afforded protection from personal liability. This type of entity works well when you have a silent partner, or partners who provide financing, but who want no say in the day-to-day operation of the business.

> Not every state treats an LLC with absolute shareholder protection. Some states, such as California, limit what type of business may be formed as an LLC, while others do not allow the "pass through" tax benefits. Perform a background search using the website for the state in which you wish to operate. Be aware that there are a number of different ownership structures available to you. Do some exploring to find out what best fits your needs.

How to Incorporate

Each state has its own registry requirement for corporations and LLC's. Generally the process begins with the selection of a unique name for that state (e.g., "Up North Getaway, LLC"). Using your unique name, file Articles of Incorporation or Organization with the state's regulatory agency. The Articles are intended to give notice to the world of the nature and the location of your company. Normally a registered agent and registered office is named to give contact information for the company. Once you file your organizing paperwork, you will need to file an Employer Identification Number (EIN) with the Internal Revenue Service, which serves essentially as a social security number for your company. You can do this online at www.irs.gov. You may have to procure a state tax number as well, by filing with the taxing authority of the state in which you incorporate. Using the EIN, you will be able to open a bank account in the name of your new company.

Each year you are required to file an annual report with the state, which confirms whether the corporation or LLC is still operating, and that the contact information is still current. The annual report does not include financial information. Your state may require additional information or filings; please consult with the proper regulatory bureau or department in your state. It is very important to maintain your corporate filings in order to continue your corporate protection: if you fail to keep up, your company could be dissolved by the state. I have had a number of clients over the years come to me and say, "I can't get a loan," or "I can't get a license," and usually it is because they have allowed their state filings to lapse. Normally the fix is easy; you can file updated reports, but it can cost money and time and create unwanted hassles. Do yourself a favor and file on time.

Maintaining the Corporate Shield

There is a concept in corporate law called "Piercing the Corporate Veil." It is used by people suing a corporation in an attempt to reach the personal assets of its shareholders. Normally, if you sue Ford Motor Company, you cannot recover against the Ford family's personal assets, only from the corporation. In dealing with large companies having a lot of assets, that is not usually an issue. When dealing with small "mom and pop" companies, it becomes a huge issue. In short, the "corporate veil" may be pierced if the corporation is not being operated as a corporate entity. In order to maintain corporate protection from personal liability, you must diligently operate as a separate entity from your personal accounts.

You cannot commingle your personal and company assets and liabilities. This is why you must open a bank account for the company, as we describe later, and use that account to take in payments and pay your company's liabilities (bills). Do not use that account to pay your personal credit card bills, or other personal items, or you could be creating unwanted liability issues. The goal is simple: keep your LLC or LP separate from your personal accounts, and you should have no problems.

When acting on behalf of the company, it is important that you clearly state that fact to third parties. When you sign correspondence or contracts in the company's name, always sign as follows:

ABC COMPANY, INC.

/s/ Your signature

By: Print your name

Its: (The capacity in which you are acting, e.g., President or Authorized Member)

This signature format clearly states that the company is making the representations or promises. You are only signing as someone who is authorized to act on behalf of the company, not as an individual. If you have business cards or a letterhead, make sure it states that the company is an incorporated entity (however you chose to set it up) and that you are only a shareholder or an officer. Now there can be no confusion as to your actions; you are working on behalf of the company, not yourself.

Having the Company Own the Property

In most if not all cases, the most valuable asset of the company will be the rental property itself. In a perfect scenario, the rental property will be owned by the company, not by you individually. This again serves to provide a legal barrier between the property and your personal assets.

Before choosing whether or not to place your property in an LLC or an LP, you must consider how the property is financed. If you own the property and there is a mortgage in your name, you cannot transfer the property to a new entity. Many mortgages have a due-on-transfer clause, which will accelerate the balance due when the property is transferred from the mortgagee to a third party, including your LLC or corporation. You must consult your mortgage lender to find out what options you may have, if any.

Vacation Rental Restrictions on Use

Many attractive destination areas have restrictive state, county, or local statutes, ordinances, or other regulations that could impact your ability to operate a short-term vacation rental.

Many of these ordinances and regulations are tailored to protect the safety and welfare of the renter and the community. Other ordinances have been passed to protect existing businesses by creating an entry barrier into the market place. Some local governments believe that the transient nature of short-term renters, and the baggage (not suitcases!) they bring with them by not being invested in the community, create unwanted problems. A number of local governments have passed restrictive zoning ordinances which prohibit renting homes on a short-term basis in certain residential areas.

Some local communities require a specific license to lease rental units to third parties. The process of obtaining the license usually includes an application, a filing fee, and an inspection. The application serves to put the community on notice that the property is being used as a rental. The inspection assures the locality and the public that the property is clean and safe. If you do not have a license in many of these localities, you cannot sue the renter for damages or evict them. While an eviction action would be extremely rare in a short-term rental, you could be subject to fines and other actions for operating an unlicensed rental. Remember that many of your renters are renting sight unseen. If you can show your renters that your property has passed an inspection, you are telling potential customers that your property has the seal of approval.

You may also find hidden restrictions to leasing your property in Home Owners Associations (HOAs) or Condominium Associations. Many of these associations are run like mini-fiefdoms with restrictive covenants on what you can and cannot do, including the ability to lease the property. Before you purchase a property, find out if it is part of an HOA or a Condominium Association. If so, discover what restrictions, if any, these groups may have. A client came to me recently after purchasing a condominium for the expressed purpose of fixing it up and leasing it, only to find out that the condominium association only allowed leasing in a small percentage of the units, and there was a long waiting list to rent them out. There was no relief available for my client, who had to sit on an empty condo and get on the waiting list as mandated by the association.

> Make sure that you are not restricted by a local association from accomplishing your goals for the property.

These types of restrictions vary from community to community, and even from block to block. You must have a clear understanding of these potential restrictions before you decide to purchase a specific property. Perform your due diligence. These restrictions may not appear in a real estate listing or in a title insurance policy commitment. Retain a local attorney to assist you in the transaction, and ask him if there are zoning or other restrictions in place; if so, are you able to get a variance or a change in the restriction to operate the vacation rental? You can contact the local city or town offices and ask what licenses or approvals are necessary to operate a vacation rental business. Look at the surrounding area and see if other properties are offered as short-term rentals. Each situation is unique; a little investigation before you buy could save you time and money down the road.

Legal Issues in Renting Your Property

Once you have purchased your vacation property, you must prepare to lease it to the renting public. To begin with, you will need to find good, respectful renters. Attracting those renters is handled in other sections of this book, but the primary legal consideration is screening prospective renters. You are inviting the public onto your private property and entrusting your renters to treat your property as if it were their own. A vast majority of all prospective renters will treat your property with respect, but you will want to pre-screen prospective renters just in case.

> If you choose to screen the applicants yourself, the most important factor is to be honest. Answer all applicants' questions with complete candor. Any promise or representation you make to the renter in order to induce them to lease the property may later be used against you.

Normal "puffing" is acceptable. For example, you may say, "It has the best sunset views in the Great Lakes," or, "It is within walking distance from the best beaches in Florida," so long as the statement is reasonably founded in reality. But if you say, "We have a great deck overlooking the water," and you do not have a deck or are not near the water, or if you say, "The unit sleeps eight" and it only sleeps four, you are making a misrepresentation that could materially affect the transaction. Should your renter be dissatisfied with their stay, they may use that misrepresentation against you.

In most cases your vacation rental will not be subject to the Fair Housing Act (FHA), the Americans with Disabilities Act (ADA), or other federal laws that traditionally regulate leasing property or that extend offers for lodging, with certain very important exceptions. If you claim in your marketing materials that your property is handicap accessible, you must comply with the ADA. If your property has common areas such as public restrooms, public parking, or a public pool, those areas must be compliant with the ADA. If your property has four or more units, then you must be ADA complaint. The federal government provides a nice primer on how to maintain ADA compliance at http://www.ada.gov/racheck.pdf. Of course, some states and local municipalities have more restrictive ordinances, which could require accessibility. Make sure you check the local laws.

Your prospective renters will frequently be strangers. The screening process is a good way to get a feeling about how a prospective renter intends to use your property. Ask the prospective renter open-ended questions about what they are looking for in a rental, and use their answers and their questions to you as clues to their intent.

Although it is likely that federal and state laws regarding discrimination in renting will not apply to your situation, it is not good policy or practice to unilaterally screen prospective renters for an immutable characteristic such as race, age, religion, national origin, or sex. If you are screening the potential renters yourself, you should screen against pre-established criteria such as the ability to pay, or the allowance of pets. If you do not feel comfortable dealing with the public, or do not have the time to book your property, management companies can be employed to manage the booking for you.

When you employ a third party service, federal laws regarding discrimination and accommodation will apply not only to the service, but to you as well.

Please find out whether your state requires management companies (or persons) to be licensed. In Michigan, the person you employ to rent and manage your property must be a licensed real estate salesperson or broker. State law requires that individuals and entities engaging in seasonal rentals for another must be licensed: An individual or entity engaged in the lease or rental of seasonal vacation properties on behalf of others, as a whole or partial vocation, and for a fee or other valuable consideration, must be licensed in accordance with Article 25 of Public Act 299 of 1980 as amended, either as a real estate broker, or as a real estate salesperson employed by a licensed real estate broker.

> Make sure that anyone you hire to book your rental follows all applicable federal, state, and local laws. You are ultimately responsible for the people you employ.

The Rental Agreement

The lease of your property to a renter is a business transaction and should be treated as such. The transaction is contractual in nature and should absolutely be memorialized in a written contract, rental agreement, or lease. For all intents and purposes they are the same thing. I will use the term "rental agreement" going forward. The rental agreement contains the relevant terms and conditions of your transaction; in particular, the dates of the rental, the address of the property, the names of the renters, the rate they are paying, when the payment is due, whether pets are allowed (and if there is an additional fee for pets), whether a security deposit is necessary and if so how much, and any other term that is vital to your agreement. If the booking is cancelled, the agreement may also be used to make deposits non-refundable or partially refundable. The rental agreement will be the ultimate record of the transaction between you and the renter; if at some point there is a disagreement over the renter's stay, you can point to the rental agreement to resolve the issue.

> You should have your attorney draft a standard rental agreement specifically tailored for your needs, which you can fill out for each new renter.

The agreement would contain all non-negotiable terms and conditions, with blank spaces for the dates of tenancy and rate. You should provide the agreement to the renter when they reserve your property, and have them sign and return the agreement when they submit their deposit. This serves to "lock-in" the renter and give you some added certainty in your reservations.

A security deposit – which is separate from the deposit to reserve the property – can be an important tool to protect a property owner from property damage caused by renters. I have a client who operates a beautiful cottage on Lake Erie. The cottage has a wrap-around deck with stunning lake views. However, the operators did not take a security deposit until one summer weekend, when their renters decided to use the gas grill on the deck. Unfortunately, the grill heated up and caused the window pane to shatter in the glassed-in back porch. After the weekend, the renters went back to their lives and my client was left with a broken window that needed quick repair before the next renter arrived. Without a security deposit the repair cost came out of their pocket, a mistake they would never make again.

> Most states have highly restrictive laws regarding the collection and application of security deposit funds because these funds, while being held by the landlord, belong to the renter until they are applied to damage of the premises.

In many states, these laws do not apply to short-term rentals. That being said, the nature of the transaction remains the same: the funds belong to the renter until they are applied to damages. If there are no specific rules in place in your state, it would be in your best interest to open an account specifically for the security deposit. Be specific in your rental agreement about how the security deposit will be handled. The security deposit cannot be applied to the costs associated with cleaning or normal wear and tear, only to damage specifically attributable to the renter. You should have a standard timeline for notifying renters of potential charges and the return of the unused portion of the security deposit.

> Remember that the security deposit is not your money until it is applied to specific charges; do not commingle it with your personal funds, or the funds of your company.

Conclusion

Real estate can be a lucrative business opportunity. However, as with any investment or business opportunity, there are perils. Protect yourself and your family by following the guidelines in this chapter.

> I will leave you with another old saying: failing to plan is a plan for failure. Consult with a local attorney who specializes in real property law in the community where you plan to operate.

Initially lawyers can be costly, but the protections they provide are worthwhile. Each aspect of your operation is subject to federal, state, and local laws, and each locality will have its own additional quirks. The information presented in this chapter is intended to give you an idea of what issues you may face in operating your vacation rental business. Perform your due diligence, and you should have no worries.

Chapter Recap

- Having a company own your investment property can protect you and your investment.
- Before purchasing a property, verify that you can rent it the way you want to! Are there any restrictions?

- Never rent your property without a rental agreement.
- You should charge a security deposit, but be careful to follow your state's security deposit laws.
- If you hire a management company to manage your vacation rental, remember that you are ultimately responsible.

The chapter strongly recommends consulting with an attorney in your state, or the state in which your vacation property resides. Legal matters can vary from state to state and even from city to city. The recommendations in this book may not be available to you, or may not be the best option for your unique situation.

Chapter 7

Setting Up Your Business

What you will learn . . .

- What you must do to set up your real estate investment business and begin renting your property
- The importance of a reliable maintenance person and cleaning person

. . . and more!

This chapter explains what you need to do to get your business up and running in order to start generating rental income.

Name Your Business and Property

Create a catchy name for your vacation rental property. This name may also be the name of your company and your website. For example, our Lakefront Chalet is called "Up North Getaway," and our Ski Condo is called "Boyne Mountain Getaway." Our business names are the same: "Up North Getaway, LLC" and "Boyne Mountain Getaway, LLC." The associated websites are "www.UpNorthGetaway.com" and "www.BoyneMountainGetaway.com". The name should grab the attention of a prospective renter and be something they will remember. Once you determine the name of your business, have your Attorney or CPA register your business name by filing the appropriate paperwork in your state. This process was explained in the previous chapter.

Create Your New Business

Contact your CPA or attorney and have them create and file the appropriate paperwork to get your Tax Identification number, and any other documents your state requires. To apply for a Tax ID Number (TIN) in Michigan, I need an Operating Agreement, the Doing Business As (DBA) filed with the State of Michigan, and my Articles of Incorporation. This may sound confusing as well as tedious, but your accountant or attorney can do it all for you in a couple days. It isn't that tough. Please consult your accountant or attorney, as these rules may differ from state to state.

Website

In order to advertise, rent, and properly manage your property, you must have a website. Creating a website for your property is extremely important, and should be one of the first things you do. Creating a website will be explained in more detail in the Advertising and Website chapters.

Phone Number

You should provide a phone number on your website, and on all of your advertising. We currently use our cell phone numbers as the main point of contact. If you do not feel comfortable using your cell phone, get a free Google phone number through Google Voice. Your Google phone number will ring into your current cell phone (or any phone you link it to), and you avoid putting your actual cell number on the internet. With Google Voice you can easily redirect the Google number to a different phone if your cell number changes, and switch the number to your home number or to your business partner's phone number. Note: you can choose any area code for your new phone number. I could choose a Google phone number with the area code at the location of the Ski Condo, so that potential renters think they are calling someone local.

Business Address

Provide a contact address for snail-mail payments and correspondence on all websites that advertise your property, including your personal website. We do not use our home address for our real estate rental businesses, because we do not want our home address on the internet for everyone to see. We use one PO Box for all of our rental property businesses. A PO Box is not a lot of money, and it keeps everything sorted out and separated from your personal mail. I recommend that you get a PO Box.

Email

If you reserve your own domain name (as explained later), you should use the email with your unique domain name. For example, I own the domain name www.boynemountaingetaway.com and my email for the business is Rentals@boynemountaingetaway.com. Doing this separates the business from my personal email, and is much more professional when dealing with renters and prospects. Instead of using trevor34x@yahoo.com, or boynemountaingetaway@yahoo.com, I use the Rentals email account for everything to do with our Ski Condo rental. Our contractors, cleaning person, maintenance person, and renters use this email address. All of our advertising uses this email address as well. I can access this email on my smart phone, and respond to rental inquires wherever I am. The goal is to keep everything centralized and easy to manage. Never use other email addresses provided by other sources such as the big national advertising sites. Keep it simple: one email for your business, and all of your advertising should point to this central email address.

Deed

Should you or shouldn't you quit claim the property out of your name and into your business name? A quit claim deed simply transfers interest or ownership in the property from you to your business. I recommend consulting your attorney, CPA, and mortgage broker for advice on this topic. It's as simple as filing a document with the register of deeds in the county where the property is located. The main reason for transferring ownership of the property from you to your company is for liability reasons. As discussed in the Financing and Legal chapters, you might have a "due on sale" clause in your mortgage on the property. If you sell or transfer the property, the lender wants their money back and will no longer want you to hold the current mortgage. I personally quit claim all of our investment properties into the LLC's of our business names. Consult with your Master Mind group and make the decision whether to do this step or not.

Insurance

If you put the property in the name of the business, you have to contact your insurance agent. More than likely, your current insurance policy only covers you, not the business. Here is what I do: after closing and after forming the business, I have the insurance policy in the name of my business and have my wife and I (the owners of the business) named as "additional insureds" on the policy. Please take the advice of your attorney and/or insurance agent. In addition, there are other items to discuss with your agent, such as loss of rents insurance, and liability insurance. Please refer to the Insurance chapter for more details on insurance.

Banking

Once you have formed your company through your CPA or attorney, it is time organize your banking. You can use a big bank or a small credit union, it doesn't matter. If you have a good existing relationship with a bank or credit union, use them. It is much easier in the long run if all your accounts are at the same bank, and linked with online banking. You do not necessarily need to have a branch of the bank where your property is located. When I bought my first vacation property, I thought I needed a branch locally at the property, but over the years I have never found a reason to use a local branch. Your existing relationship with a bank is more important than its physical location.

After determining the bank you will use, call the bank and ask them what is required to open a business account. In Michigan, I need a copy of our Operating Agreement, the Articles of Incorporation, and the document for my Tax ID Number. Take the required documents to your bank, open a business checking account, and sign up for online banking. Be prepared to deposit/transfer money into your new business account. The amount is up to you and the math for your property; you might want to seed the business with $500 to $5,000.

Make sure everyone that should have access to the accounts is there to sign the documents. You will get a starter set of checks and you can either order more from your bank or get them online at places like www.vistaprint.com. Get a debit card and a credit card for you and your business partners.

When I open my business accounts, I apply for the credit card at the same time. Getting a credit card for a new company can be difficult, and an existing relationship might come in handy. Now let me explain in more detail what you need in your banking toolbox.

- *Checkbook.* I know, using checks is becoming a thing of the past, but they still serve a business purpose. From time to time you many need to pay a contractor, maintenance guy, refund a renter, or pay the cleaning person on the spot. You will need a checkbook on your checking account and access for all signers on the account.
- *Online Banking.* We pay 95% of our bills online. It is easy to set up "Payees" and "Recurring Payments" such as the mortgage payment and utilities. Online banking also makes it very easy on your accountant at the end of the year. Every online banking account I have ever had allows you to download your transactions, which you can give to your accountant. All of our personal and business accounts are with the same bank and are linked online. If we need money in one of our business accounts, we can easily transfer it from our personal account via online banking.
- *Debit Card.* You may need a debit card to pull cash out of an ATM; i.e., to pay a contractor or buy supplies. You can also use it in place of the credit card if you have to, but I would only use it at big reputable stores such as Home Depot. I don't use it for anything else because if someone took the numbers off my debit card, they could drain my checking account. I have been told that fraudulent charges to a credit card can be reversed in less than 24 hours, but it can take weeks to get your money back into your debit card account.
- *Credit Card.* Credit cards do not exist to charge up and keep a balance! Use this card for everything associated with the business, but remember that you should pay it off at the end of the

month. We use our credit card for expenses, which are discussed in the Accounting chapter. We purchase all supplies, equipment, new furniture, and everything for the property with the credit card. Why? It is extremely easy to use, all businesses accept credit cards, and we (and you) will buy a lot of supplies and items online. Many credit card companies have end-of-year reports that list on what and where you spent your money. These reports allow your accountant to easily track your yearly expenses. If the credit card number is stolen you can report the theft, and you may not be on the hook for fraudulent charges. Lastly, a credit card makes it very easy to keep all purchases for the property separated from your normal day-to-day living expenses.

> Never use your personal checking or savings accounts to pay bills or expenses associated with the rental property. If there is no money in your business account, transfer money from your personal account into the business account and pay the bill from the business account.

Maintenance

> It could be argued that a reliable local maintenance person and a reliable cleaning person are the two most important factors that make this real estate investing model work.

Finding a reliable maintenance person or company is very important, and should be investigated when you begin to look at properties. Ask other owners, neighbors, and real estate agents for the phone numbers of handymen/maintenance persons. Interview them and find out what they can and cannot do. For bigger tasks, ask them if they have contacts who specialize in plumbing, HVAC (furnace and A/C), and electrical. Once you find a maintenance person, explain that from time to time you are going to call them out of the blue to QUICKLY respond to a problem or an issue at your property. In other words, tell them that they will be "on call." Tell them you will try not to bother them after working hours, but that they will be the main contact for all maintenance issues you have at your property. Establish a base hourly rate or other terms that both of you agree on. The rate will depend on their level of experience and the area/market you are in.

At one of my properties I pay my maintenance man $25 per hour for quick jobs, and negotiate the larger ones by the job. I am very fair with our maintenance guys because I want them to be very happy with us, and to drop what they are doing and respond to our requests. Sometimes they will fix things for free, but we never accept that. Instead, while at the property we invite them over for dinner, or we send them a gift card for Applebee's or a similar restaurant, to surprise and thank them for their help. Always treat your maintenance guys as if they were doing you a favor, even though you are paying them. Because they are!

Here's a strong suggestion: ask anyone who visits your property to perform any type of work for a copy of their insurance documents. This would include, but not necessarily be limited to, Worker's Compensation (Workman's Comp) and General Liability insurance. These were explained in the Inspection chapter. You want your inspector to be insured, and contractors who work at your property should also have their own coverage.

Next, while visiting your property and throughout the year, bring your property checklist and take a quick look around to ensure that everything is going smoothly. Peruse the free checklists in the references section on GetawayX.com. Make sure that your property stays in great shape for you and your renters!

Finally, just like your automobile, every property has recommended and routine maintenance. If you never change your oil, your engine will eventually seize up and cost you thousands of dollars to repair. The same goes for your rental property. It amazes me how many property owners do not service their HVAC/furnace each year. Some tell me that they don't want to spend the money, but I say that is hogwash.

You must maintain the property for this strategy to be successful. Everything must work correctly, and you don't want to worry about something going wrong while you have a renter renting your property. Yearly maintenance on some items inside and outside the property should mitigate future issues with the property. A sample checklist can be downloaded from GetawayX.com.

Cleaning

Again, it could be argued that a reliable local maintenance person and a reliable cleaning person are the two most important factors that make this real estate investing model work. Don't take this lightly!

Your property must be as clean and fresh smelling as if it was brand new. Therefore, you need an extremely reliable person to clean your property between renters. You can hire a local person or company to do this for you, but make sure to have a back-up cleaning person. I have always used individuals, not cleaning companies, for our properties. Finding a cleaning person is not that difficult. Ask the real estate agent who helped you buy the property to refer a cleaning person. If you have owned the property for a while and are just now turning it into a rental, call a local real estate office, talk to an agent, and ask them for some names of cleaning people. You can also ask other vacation rental owners around your property. Always keep your eyes open. When we were looking to buy the Ski Condo, and while we were seeing other properties for sale, we ran into two cleaning ladies. We got their business cards and when we bought our Ski Condo we invited both of them over to chat, and selected one of them. At our Lakefront Chalet it wasn't that easy. We asked the wait staff at local restaurants for referrals and our real estate agent for advice. We finally went with a cleaning person the agent recommended, and she has been with us for thirteen years.

You will need to personally interview potential cleaning persons. Give them a list of what you expect to be done every time between renters, the one-time yearly clean, and the periodic cleaning touch-ups when there is down time between rentals. Dust can collect if a month goes by without anyone in the property, and a periodic clean-up creates a fresh-smelling property just before a renter checks in.

Don't try too hard to negotiate a cheap rate with the cleaning person. Remember, this person can make or break your success. I know that we pay more than we should to clean one of our properties, but I don't care because she is always there when we need her, even at the last minute. If I tried to beat her up on price, do you really think she would go out of her way for me in the future?

Determine what supplies you will provide and what the cleaner will provide. At the Ski Condo we provide the vacuum, and she provides all of the other cleaning supplies. At the Lakefront Chalet, we provide everything needed to clean (vacuum, mop, bucket, sponges, and cleaners). We keep everything in the supplies closet at the property. There is a suggested checklist on GetawayX.com.

Lastly, when you stay at your property do not clean it yourself. You can lightly clean and tidy up, but make sure to have your cleaning person come in and do a professional clean before the next renters come in.

Property Guide

Provide a guide at your property for your renters. There is simply too much information to cover on the phone before their trip. After you enter your property data on your GetawayX website, you can print your guide and leave it at your property, along with a link to it on your website. Having your guide online is a must! If a renter has a question they can simply go to your website via their smart phone and get the answer. At a minimum, your guide should include the following information:

- Medical information. Phone numbers and directions to the nearest hospital and ambulance.
- The address of the rental property, major crossroads, and local landmarks.
- Emergency numbers. Your contact phone numbers, the local Fire and Police numbers, and any others the renter might need. Do not give renters the phone numbers of your cleaning person or maintenance person. The renter should call you and only you with an issue, and you will call the cleaning person or maintenance person if you deem it necessary. Never allow your renters access to your contractors and Master Mind group.
- The location of the First Aid kit and the fire extinguishers.
- The common closet and the items in it.
- The location of the cleaning supplies.
- How to operate items such as electronics, appliances, and equipment; the DVD player, the TV, the fireplace, the hot tub, the oven, the shower, thermostats, special instructions (no garbage disposal, no fish cleaning), garbage pick-up day, the coffee maker, and where to find appliance manuals.
- Who to call if the power goes out; i.e., call power company first and then call you.
- Your rules: no smoking, no pets, check in-check out time.
- If your property is a condo or association, mention their rules.
- Parking information.

- How to access your internet/WiFi if you provide it.

In addition to the items listed above, the following information can be included, depending on how detailed you want to be: local attractions and calendar of local events, directions to the best/nearest grocery store(s), information on and menus for local restaurants, information on shopping, directions to the nearest temples, churches, and airport. Most of this information can be listed on your website under the Local Area tab.

Your property guide should be as detailed as is appropriate for the area. The Ski Condo is located at a large ski resort, and everyone who goes up there can easily get information about the area on the internet, as well as by stopping at the resort's front desk. Our property guide therefore just provides basic information. In contrast, we provide a very detailed guide on the local area for our Lakefront Chalet, because it is located in the middle of nowhere. A property guide is a "nice-to-have," so don't lose sleep over it. At minimum, provide the information above on your website, and leave a print-out at your property for the renters.

Keys

Even if you live in the area of your vacation rental, the easiest way to get renters into your property is through a lockbox. Call the renter before their trip and go over the check-in procedures, and provide the lockbox code that contains the key to open the door. To avoid lockouts, tell your renters to put the key back in the lockbox after they open the door. Provide a couple more keys in the kitchen (or wherever is convenient) next to your property guide. Mount two key lockboxes at your property – you should have a backup in case the renters lock themselves out. It is also a good idea to give a key to your maintenance person and/or cleaning person, or to a neighbor you trust who is willing to hold a backup key for you. If the renters lock themselves out of both lockboxes, you will have a third back up to let them in. It is 100 percent your fault if your renters get locked out! Make sure a plan is in place to prevent a ruined vacation. We use the same code for both lockboxes and change the code once every year. If you can, try not to use lockboxes that hang on the door handle. Over time, they damage the doors by being bounced around, and they also loosen the door handles. Currently we use a "wall mounted key storage box," which you can find online or at a local hardware store for around $20 to $30. See pictures of two types of mounted lockboxes below.

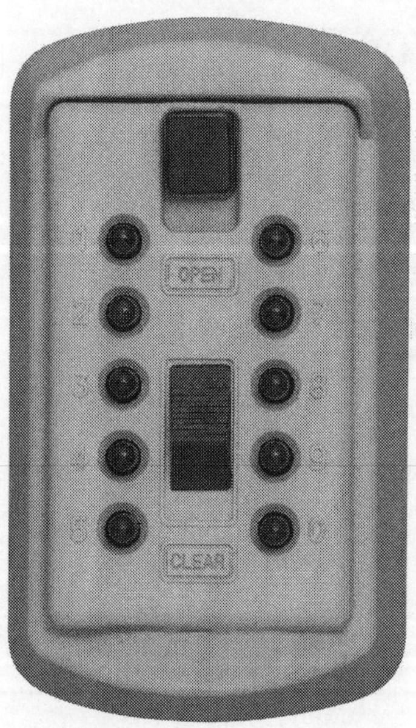

Lockboxes come in many different types, including complex electronic ones that store random codes, and ones you can access from the internet. In the end, it is up to you to choose what works best for your situation.

We have never had a stolen or copied key, or a break in. Think about it: if someone were to break into our Ski Condo, the only items to steal are the TVs and the furniture. Who is going to go through all that trouble to steal a couch? TVs are so cheap now, who wants to steal a $150 TV?

The same for our Lakefront Chalet. You will not have anything of real value in your rental property, and so no motivation for key stealing or breaking in.

Some vacation rental owners are overly concerned with security and do not even give the codes to their cleaning person or maintenance person. Eventually you realize that you must trust people - especially your maintenance and cleaning person. If you can't trust them with a key or the code, they are not the right people for you. Over the years our maintenance and cleaning people have become friends. We treat them right and they treat us right. Similarly for our renters; we now have a lot of repeat renters, and we don't worry about lockbox codes.

Tracking Your Income and Expenses

Tracking your income and expenses is not difficult. Just remember that if you spend money associated with the property, use the property's checkbook, online banking, debit card, or credit card. Some owners keep a written ledger of income and expenses, and some keep the information electronically. You do not need to buy special software to keep track of your property's income and expenses. In the chapter about computing the math, I only listed thirteen potential expenses and one income stream (your rental income). You don't need a Masters degree in accounting and a super computer! If you use your business credit card, business checks, and your property's online business banking, the bank statements and reports will keep track of everything for you online. Utilize the tools your bank offers, and ask your accountant how he or she wants this information at the end of the year.

Check-in and Check-out Procedures

Set a procedure for check-in and check-out, but always be flexible and work with your renters. Monitor what your competition does and what is typical for your area. We typically rent weekends Friday-Sunday, with check-in at 4 p.m. and check-out at 11 a.m.; and weekly Sunday-Sunday check-in at 4 p.m. and check-out at 11 a.m. This gives our cleaning person a five-hour window to clean between renters. Renting Sunday to Sunday allows you to squeeze in a Friday-Sunday weekend rental just before a weekly rental.

Pet Policy

It is your choice to allow dogs, cats, and other pets in your rental. Our policy has always been not to accept pets. Over my many years of renting homes, animals more often than not have caused damage, messes, or have interfered with the allergies of the next renters. My wife is a big animal lover. We attend a charity auction every year to help support sick animals, and we donate money and supplies to animal charities and no-kill shelters. We have nothing against animals; we love them. However, we are running a vacation rental business that must be clean and allergen-free for all renters. We have never failed to rent our properties because we do not accept pets. Our policy is: "We are sorry, but pets are not permitted because we have to provide a clean environment for people that may be allergic to cat and/or dog hair. We wish to provide a clean and healthy atmosphere for all of our guests."

Decorating and Furnishings

Some basic rules:

- Know your clientele before redecorating or furnishing your vacation rental. What type of people will your property attract? What do your potential renters expect? After a day of skiing, our Ski Condo renters expect a nice, modern, clean, simple place to stay that has a switch to turn on the gas fireplace, and WiFi internet access. At the Lakefront Chalet, the renters expect a more rustic setting; they want a natural fireplace and a "cottage in the woods" décor. We have never had WiFi access there – our clients prefer seclusion.

- The furnishings and items in your property will eventually become ruined, stained, broken, or lost. Do not leave anything that means a lot to you. And do not buy a white couch!

- During the first few years of renting, I recommend keeping things simple and updating the property slowly as the years go by. Give yourself time to think about how you want to decorate for the long-term.

- Think practically, not with grand design dreams – don't become emotionally attached to the property right off the bat. Your goal is to make the property rentable; it is not yet your dream vacation home. Once you get a steady flow of trusted, repeat renters, or after it is paid off and you can pull back on the rentals, then you can renovate and decorate to your personal tastes.

- Always think from a renter's point of view. Think of what you would want and expect if you were renting the property as a vacationer.

- Try to update the property once a year with a new carpet, a new couch, new ceiling fan(s), paint, area rugs, a new radio, new pots and pans. Every year we make an improvement to our properties. Repeat renters notice them, and always comment how much they appreciate that we care enough about the property to keep improving it. This creates repeat renters who want to rent from you again.

Now that you have the basic rules, let's discuss them in more detail. When you first buy your property, you will probably be very excited to decorate and make it your dream home. Try not to go overboard right away! Start by getting the property in just enough shape to rent and cater to your target renters. Your property should at least show to the level of your competition, and you should provide amenities to the standards of your competition. Then try to take it up a notch to make yourself stand out.

When friends and family heard that we bought our first vacation home, a lot of offers came in. "Hey we're buying a new couch, coffee table, end table, bed, (etc.), could you use our old one up at your new vacation property?" Always entertain the idea because it's free! However, try to not let the place look like a hodge-podge of unmatched garage sale items. We definitely took up offers on free furniture, but we tried our best to keep the items looking good together. Don't forget, an inexpensive couch slipcover from Bed Bath and Beyond can make that hand-me down couch any color you need it to be! Also, the slipcover can be easily taken off and washed, or replaced much less expensively than buying a new couch. Think out of the box to save some money!

Don't overdo it! Whatever you do, don't go to Ethan Allen or Pottery Barn and buy a brand new expensive couch or table. At the Lakefront Chalet, we are on our third sofa and second dining room set in only thirteen years! At all our rental properties, dining room chairs are the first to break, and couches become worn out and stained. Our current couch is an 'L' shaped couch from Costco we bought for $600 – a brown microfiber that is easily cleaned. We have had it for five years now, and it still looks brand new. One more note on sofas: paying just a little more money can get you a sofa/sleeper combination with a hide-away bed, which means your property now can sleep two more people! That can lead to more rent money! The same thing goes for pots and pans, dishes, cups, and so on. Don't buy expensive, pretty, colorful plates to match the kitchen décor. After many chipped plates and cups, we finally replaced them with Corelle dinnerware in a simple pattern. Three years later there are still no chips, and all the plates are accounted for. If you were renting, would you prefer to see pretty dishes that were chipped, or plain basic white plates that looked brand new? Think practically: your dinnerware is going to get banged around.

The goal should be to fit in to the area, and the property should look just as you would expect if you were renting it. Then try to add a few other features that others don't have. Shop wisely: many items are cheaper online and can be shipped directly to your cleaning person or maintenance person who can take the items to the property for you.

Overall, neutral décor is better. You are not going to get a lot more rent by having custom fancy painted walls than just normal walls with neutral colors. The same goes for granite counter tops. They are beautiful but expensive, and will probably help you rent the place faster than normal. However, you will not to be able to charge much more in rent. A weekend vacationer won't care that much if your countertops are granite or linoleum.

> Always keep your property in good condition. When you notice worn or broken items, fix or replace them ASAP.

Over time you will learn what to buy and what not to buy. For example, we bought a high-end coffee maker for our Lakefront Chalet, thinking that it would be a nice touch and that people would really like it. Well, our renters and friends both said it was hard to use. We promptly replaced it with a simple $30 coffee maker, and everyone was happy.

Lesson learned. You can have nice things in your property if you like, but don't make them complex and hard to use. Keep everything simple.

Don't decorate the property with a lot of personal items and pictures of you and your family. It is OK to have a few personal pictures if they are appropriate and fit in with the décor.

For example, at our Lakefront Chalet a couple of collages have fishing pictures of friends and family that date back to the 1970s. However, these pictures are in the lower-level game room, not in the main living area.

You don't want your renters to feel that they are staying in someone else's house. Keep personal items in your owner's closet; do not leave personal belongings out in the common areas. You want your rental property to look clean, fresh, and free of clutter for the next renter.

Keep your kitchen fully stocked. See the recommended list of kitchen items on GetawayX.com. The list is large, but chances are that 90% of it is already there if the property you are purchasing is already a vacation rental property. As you visit the property and settle in for your own weekend trips, you will notice what you need above and beyond the list I have provided. Provide dishwasher-safe kitchen items to make it easier for you and your renters.

Don't rush to decorate your dream property. Only after we had 80 percent of our renters as repeat renters did we decided to fully renovate our property. We gutted the kitchen and baths and upgraded all of the flooring. The reason for waiting is that it took several years to get to know many of our repeat renters, and to trust them. All of our renters loved what we did with the place, and to this day they thank us for letting them rent from us!

Amenities

Check out your competition to see what amenities renters will expect. You can easily do this by looking at the websites of your competitors, and on advertising websites, to see the amenities offered by comparable properties. Our cleaning lady, who cleaned several other Ski Condos like ours, told us what we needed to provide to our renters. Amenities can include table games, radio/CD/iPod players, DVD players in bedrooms for kids to watch movies, internet access/WiFi, TVs, cable or satellite channels, a hot-tub, shampoo, bath soap, bath towels, and so on.

Some areas will be easier than others to determine the level of your competition. At our Lakefront Chalet we discovered that providing toiletries, morning coffee, or bath towels was unnecessary. Some of our competition didn't even provide pillows and linens! But at the Ski Condo, renters expect a hotel environment because that's how everyone else does it, and because there is a lodge/hotel at the ski hill. We have to provide bath towels, bath soap, little shampoos, conditioner, lotion, coffee, sugar, creamer, and stirrers. We purchased these items online in bulk, inexpensively. The cleaning person provides linens and bath towels because she does the same for eight other units.

Vacation rental owners are split on whether to provide a phone for their renters. At our Lakefront Chalet, we have never installed a landline phone, and no renter has ever questioned it. In this day and age almost everyone has a cell phone, and I do not see the need to provide a phone on the property. On the other hand, our Ski Condo has a phone installed in the unit and it is linked to the main lodge so that renters can call for a shuttle, book a reservation at the lodge restaurant or spa, or inquire about lodge activities. I did not install the phone, rather it was part of the condo and every condo there has one. Follow the lead of other properties in the area. If you don't need a phone, don't install one because your renters will call local, long distance, international, and collect 900 numbers.

Supplies Closet

Provide a locked closet for your cleaning person's supplies. At the Lakefront Chalet, we provide all cleaning supplies and extra linens. At the Ski Condo, the closet is full of little hotel-sized shampoos, soaps, and coffee. The cleaning person provides all the linens and towels and uses her own supplies. We also keep a simple tool kit in the supplies closet for easy fix jobs. To buy cleaning supplies in bulk go to Costco or Sam's Club, and use their coupons. A suggested list of supplies closet items can be found on GetawayX.com.

Owner's Closet

Leave one closet locked for your personal items such as personal bath and hand towels, pillows, blankets, toiletries, jackets, flashlights, rain gear, games, sports equipment (i.e., skis, ski boots, and so on). An owner's closet is convenient for you, and prevents having to pack a ton of stuff every time you visit your vacation property. Pick a closet that will not overly impact the renters. You can place an armoire in the room or a basic clothes rack. The armoire looks much nicer, but both will work, and it depends on your property. At the Lakefront Chalet a clothes rack is fine, but the Ski Condo demands the armoire.

Guest Book

A lot of vacation property owners love the idea of a guest book. I have never had one at any of my properties, and I never intend to have one. I don't see the point of having one and I do not see the value it adds. I have never had a problem renting any of my properties without a guest book, and I have a lot of repeat renters. During the past twelve years, nobody has ever asked me where my guest book was – nobody cares. But I will leave this up to you. If you decide to use a guest book, look online for information on best practices. Keep in mind that a guest book is just something else you need to keep track of, and to keep clean and undamaged.

Chapter Recap

- Think of a great name for your business and website – your BRAND.
- Set up your insurance and banking.
- Make agreements with a maintenance man/company and a cleaning person/company. These two people can make or break your success.
- Find a reliable local maintenance person and a reliable cleaning person. Don't take this lightly!
- Provide décor, furnishings, and amenities at the level of other property owners in the area, geared to what renters will expect, and then take it up a notch.
- Be realistic and practical with furnishings and décor. Over time, things may get damaged.
- Always keep items in good condition. When you notice something wearing out or that is broken, fix or replace it ASAP.
- Set the property up for both yourself and the renter, by setting aside an "owners closet" for yourself.
- You might want to provide a Property Guide, but skip the Guest Book!

Chapter 8

Advertising

What you will learn . . .

- The number one method of advertising – focus on repeat renters
- The many avenues to advertise your rental property

. . . and more!

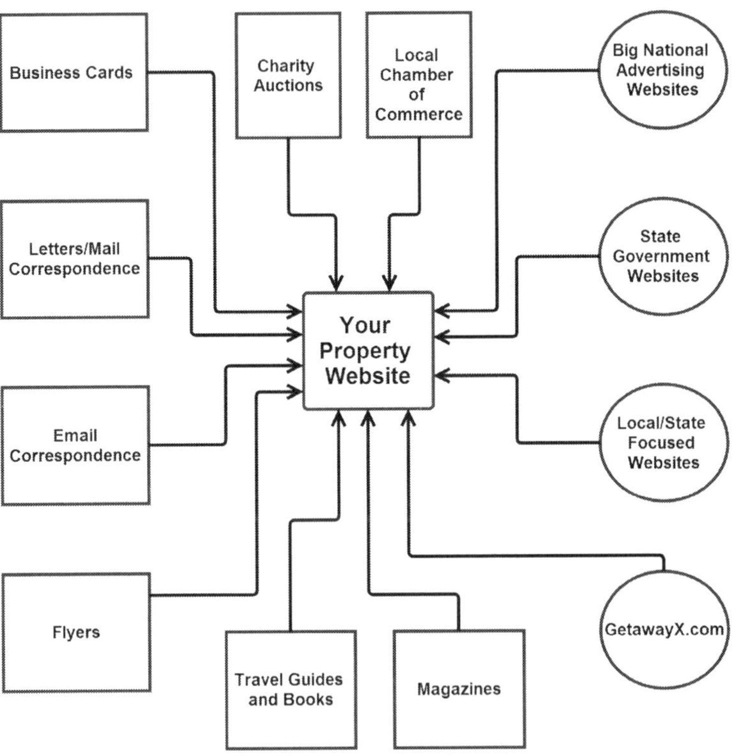

Figure 8.1: How to Advertise Your Property

Over the years I have applied many different advertising methods and have learned what works and what doesn't. Advertising is the way to get people to rent your property, and you must take this seriously. Track the source of your inquiries so you know where your advertising dollars are best spent. When someone inquires about your property, ask them how they heard of you. Tracking your advertising will allow you to spend your advertising dollars wisely. There are four basic advertising channels everyone should use, and from there you have to think out of the box for the advertising that will best fit your area. The four main advertising channels are: 1) your own website, 2) your list of previous renters and people who have inquired about your property, 3) nationwide advertising, and 4) local advertising.

I have owned vacation properties for a decade, but it was only in the last two years that I began to use a national advertising website, and only for the Ski Condo. That's right: I have never advertised our Lakefront Chalet on ANY of the big national advertising websites, and I have no problem renting it. I am not saying that you shouldn't use them, but rather that there are many effective ways to advertise your property for rent. Don't stop short by only using the big national advertising sites.

Existing Renters

Have your real estate agent ask the seller for a list of people to whom the sellers have rented the property, and the people who have inquired about renting the property in the past. As I will explain later, you will market to past renters and to those who have inquired about renting. Get as many of the details as possible: names, email, phone numbers, dates rented, amount of rent paid, how many years they have rented from the seller . . . and anything else the seller will provide. Send an email or letter to the previous renters, introducing yourself as the new owner, and possibly offering them a discount to rent the property again.

Sales Pitch and Description

Come up with a quick and easy but catchy explanation of your property, only a couple sentences long. Most forms of advertising you will use requires a short description of your rental property. The sales pitch for the Ski Condo is: "Located on the Disciples slope – the chair lift is right out the backdoor! Truly a SKI-IN SKI-OUT condo! 5 bedrooms / 5 full baths." The Lakefront Chalet's is: "Relax at Up North Getaway, a lakefront chalet in northwest Michigan. Nestled in the Manistee National Forest, the chalet sleeps 18 and is located just south of M-55 between Cadillac and Manistee on all-sports Pine Lake!" These are short and to the point, and people know quickly what to expect.

Next, write an effective description of your property, a few paragraphs in length, talking up your property and the area. Many vacation rental marketing books and papers tell you, in great length, all the tips and tricks of writing a great description to "sell" your property on the main advertising sites. I have never read any of them, and I have been extremely successful getting renters from my advertising descriptions.

My secret? I looked at my competition online, and on all of the big national advertising websites, and read how property owners like me described their properties. From there I wrote my own that would compete with the ones I found online.

That's it: pretty easy. Keep it simple.

Ski Condo Description:

> ** PREMIER LOCATION **
>
> Truly a SKI-IN SKI-OUT condo!
>
> Email or call now to book your trip!
>
> PLEASE NOTE! Go to our website for rates and availability: http://www.boynemountaingetaway.com
>
> Located on the Disciples slope – the chair lift is right out the backdoor! Truly a SKI-IN SKI-OUT condo! This condo consists of 2 units. The entire condo has 5 bedrooms and 5 full baths. Rent one unit or both!
>
> The upper unit is 3 bedrooms, 3 full bathrooms; master suite with king size bed and private bath, second bedroom has 2 queen size

beds and the upstairs bedroom has 2 queen size beds with private bath. Foyer, bathroom, full kitchen, and family room. Max occupancy 10.

The lower unit is 2 bedrooms, 2 full bathrooms; each bedroom has 2 double size beds. Full kitchen and family room. Max occupancy 8.

Experience some of the best golf, skiing, and snowboarding in Michigan. Enjoy the largest indoor water park in Michigan, Avalanche Bay! After tackling the Zipline, get a nice spa treatment at the Solace Spa. Exciting dining and nightlife caps off an action packed day!

There are many other places to visit and things to do within minutes of the condo. Take the ferry to Mackinac Island, visit the towns of Traverse City, Charlevoix, and Petoskey, or just relax on the beaches of Lake Michigan!

Availability calendar: http://www.boynemountaingetaway.com

List of Renters and Prospects

Having repeat renters is the low-stress way to operate your business. However, this is where most vacation property owners have trouble. They are more concerned with getting "good reviews" on their property, and paying to advertise on all the big national websites. You should continue to advertise to get renters, but you should concentrate a lot more on those renters who have previously rented from you.

The easiest and best way to get more rentals is to market to the people that have previously rented your property. The best renter is a repeat renter. You know that they paid in full, you didn't have any problems with them, they took care of your property, and you know what to expect from them.

Renters like to come back to a place where they know what to expect. Wouldn't you, if you were them? If you went on vacation and had a great experience renting a property, on your next vacation would you rather stay at the same place, or take your chances on a different property? For over a decade, prior to buying our Lakefront Chalet, my dad and I booked the same cottage up north in Michigan for our yearly fishing trip. I cannot stress this enough: previous renters should be your main focus!

Keep track of who has rented from you in the past, and anyone who has sent you an inquiry. I keep every inquiry because the potential renter took the time to call, and must have liked something about our property. Just because it wasn't available doesn't mean you should forget about these people!

Keep a log of all your previous renters AND prospects (those who inquired but who did not book.) If you utilize the GetawayX.com website and reservation system, most of this will be taken care of for you.

Mail a generic (non-religious) holiday card in December to all of your previous renters. A lot of our renters have commented on this, and some send us an email saying thanks for the card. This simple gesture keeps us in front of our target market. A couple times a year we send all of our previous renters (and prospects) a quick-to-the-point email about a discount, or something special, to get them to book a date. We inform them of any improvements at the property, and always offer repeat renters a discount. You should as well.

In addition, sending an email six months prior brings in rentals! Our Ski Condo books up completely by October 1st for ski season. There are typically some weekdays available, so we send an email in October, telling previous renters that the weeks are discounted. We also put a headline on our website, saying that weekdays are discounted. Come January, we send out an email to remind them to book for the summer, and that if they book now they will get a discount.

At GetawayX you are able to easily download your renter data to your desktop. Use that file to generate mailing labels, print letters, and to send emails and announcements targeting your list of renters. Once you get a good base of repeat renters, you can save a lot of money by cutting down on your other advertising methods. If you are looking for a free and easy method to email a large distribution list, mailchimp.com is free. I know people who use it and are happy with it.

Create a Website

Some "vacation rental advice" says that you do not need your own website for your rental property. Moreover, the big national advertising websites will never tell you that you need your own website. Most of the literature on this topic will tell you that it is expensive, time consuming, and difficult to create your own website. I completely disagree and would not invest in vacation real estate unless I had my own website. It's a MUST to have a unique website for your vacation rental; my method doesn't work without one. Check out our unique websites at www.upnorthgetaway.com, or www.boynemountaingetaway.com. These websites are all about branding!

Create your own brand that people will remember. Your unique website will be your MAIN PORTAL for everything; it is your main spot to "sell" potential renters on your property. It has a reservation system, your availability calendar, your avenue for relaying information to potential renters, and the ability to collect payments. All other advertising channels will point potential renters back to your main website.

Think about it! What would happen if you did not have your own main website, and you advertised on three different online advertising websites? You would have to constantly update three availability calendars and manage three listings. That is a lot of work, and could lead to errors and duplicate bookings.

Some contend that advertising on a big national website is all that is needed for their presence on the web. It is true that these national websites give you a web presence, but that presence is typically limited to a one-page listing, not a fully functional website. I use a large national advertising site, but my advertisement points everyone to my website for more information and for booking. And that is all you should use it for as well. Why? Because national websites advertise and drive people to my website, so that I can sell them on my property on my website. My website is my brand. When you tell someone your website name, do you really want to say "www.xzyvacationrentalsxyz.com/propertyID34681a", or does "www.upnorthgetaway.com" sound better? What's more catchy? In addition, you can do a lot more "selling" on your own website than a one-page listing on an advertising website.

The two biggest reasons not to use big national advertising sites, or similar websites, as your primary website is 1) in a few years you will not need them as much, and 2) you need a central point of contact for your property, including your availability calendar. If you make other websites your primary place of referral, you will be paying them a fee every year for the rest of your life. In my experience, you should have repeat renters after just one year renting your vacation property. As the years go by you will not need to advertise as much. Currently, I spend nothing advertising the Lakefront Chalet. I still rent to many of the same renters who have been with us since 2002, and a lot of our other repeat renters came from referrals.

The other reason not to use an advertising site as your main presence is your availability calendar. When you begin this process you WILL be advertising on multiple sites – some smaller sites customized for your specific area, and the big national ones. On which sites are you going to have your availability calendar? What if you advertise on four websites? Where do you point people to check if the date they want is available? Are you going to update all four sites all the time? No, of course not! I know that some of these advertising sites will sync their calendars with each other, but chances are that not every company you advertise with will sync with everyone else. Instead, say something like this on all of the websites you advertise on: "For more details and the availability calendar go to our main website www.upnorthgetaway.com to book your trip!" Point everyone back to your property website and have everything happen there.

The power of the internet brings people from all over the world to your vacation rental. As mentioned before, you have to come up with a catchy name for your rental. This name will not only be the name of your rental, it will be the name of your company and your website. My wife chose our business names, Up North Getaway, and Boyne Mountain Getaway. They are catchy and tell the person where they are. I would suggest something catchy and meaningful for your vacation rental. At GetawayX.com you can search for available website names. If the one you want is taken, please don't name it www.upnorthgetaway12.com. Adding random characters like "12" is not recommended, because no one will remember your website name if it has random numbers or letters in it. Avoid using dashes and weird characters, unless they have meaning to your property. Stick with a ".com" address and make it really easy to remember so you don't have to explain or spell it to people when telling them your website name.

We disclose everything on our website including the rates, dates available, and the rental agreement! After visiting our site there are very few additional questions that need answering. Our site allows people to determine whether they want to rent our properties without calling us with a lot of questions. Our website cuts out a lot of wasted time on the phone and in email.

At GetawayX.com you have the ability to create a custom website for your property. It has an online reservation system, an availability calendar, and payment processing; in short, everything you need to execute this strategy. You must only pay for your personal domain name, which is your 'www.mysitename.com', your brand. I have nothing to do with this fee, and no control over it. After paying your domain name fee to the company that issues your domain name, you will own that website address for the number of years you paid for. All of this will be further explained in the Website chapter.

National and State Focused Advertising Websites

Now that you have your own custom website for your property, the next step is to advertise your property to the world so that people will come to your new website, contact you, and book their trip! The most effective way to advertise is via online advertising websites. Go to Google and pretend to search for a vacation rental like the one you just purchased. See what comes up!

On the first page of the Google search results you will see the websites these properties are advertising on. Click these links and make a note of how many properties like yours are on that advertising website. When you find a lot of properties like yours on one of these websites, make a note of the website name. Homeaway and their consortium of websites such as VRBO, is the largest of all vacation rental advertising websites. Next, go to Homeaway and their affiliated websites (VRBO) and search for properties like yours in your area.

Between your Google search and your Homeaway search, you should easily see where to advertise: where everyone else that has a property like yours advertises. When someone does a search on the internet for your type of vacation rental, the links will more than likely point to the site where most of those properties are listed for rent.

In addition to the big national advertising websites, choose to advertise on a more localized state website. Often these sites are a lot cheaper than the big national ones. In the past we advertised our Lakefront Chalet with www.rentalbug.com for a couple years, and had a lot of rental inquiries through them. I am sure you can find a comparable state-focused website in your neck of the woods. Just make sure to advertise with a reputable website; there is no need to advertise on every random vacation rental website out there. Many of these random sites are free, but they could be shady, or scams. Use your head: if it looks odd, don't post on it.

We point people to our main website for more information, and to book their trip, on every advertising site we use.

Chamber of Commerce and City/Township Websites

When we first started advertising the Lakefront Chalet, we were members of the Chamber of Commerce of the nearest big city, and advertised on the local township website. The Lakefront Chalet is off the beaten path, and people who vacation there probably would look at the Chamber of Commerce and the local township website to see what lodgings are available. For a small yearly fee we were included in the "Lodging" section of their local chamber and township websites, as well as all locally printed advertising with links to our website. That's how we got our bookings.

State Government Websites

Every state in the US advertises their state as a great vacation destination to the world. We advertise our rentals on www.michigan.org, and it is free. Our listing with the State of Michigan has some brief catchy information; and, you guessed it, on the listing we point people to our main website for more information, and to book their trip.

Property Reviews

Most online advertising websites allow users to comment and review your vacation rental property. Online reviews of anything are always taken with some caution. People are not stupid: studies show that there are fake reviews on everything from vacation properties to toasters.

Have you ever bought a car at a dealership, or had maintenance performed on your car at a dealership? Chances are they gave you a review survey to fill out afterwards, and told you that the dealership needed good marks. Whenever we had a bad experience at a dealership, the dealer would give us a free oil change if we gave them a good review on their survey. Many reviews don't reflect reality or the truth, and most people take them with some caution.

I have never had reviews on any of my properties, and I prefer not to have any. In my opinion, reviews make no difference whatsoever in your success with my method. A lot of current vacation rental owners would probably disagree with me. However, my Ski Condo has a ton of competition. There are 116 condos in my complex almost exactly like mine. The main lodge has 220 hotel rooms, and a smaller lodge on the property also has hotel rooms. There are other rental condo complexes at the base of the ski hill, and homes for rent scattered on and around the ski hill. I have zero property reviews, yet with my method, the Ski Condo is completely booked six months before peak season. As for my Lakefront Chalet, it is in the middle of nowhere. Most people have never heard of the city it is in, and I have no issues renting it.

Success with my model is based on previous renters - people who are already loyal to you and your brand. Soliciting online reviews serves only to attract new renters - the people least loyal to you. If you are seriously concerned about online reviews, and think that reviews will make or break your success, you are going about it the wrong way. Online reviews, just like guest books, are useless.

Flyers and Business Cards

To promote the Lakefront Chalet I used vistaprint.com to design and print business cards and flyers. You just need some basic information on this advertising, and to point them to your main website. After printing the cards and flyers, I requested local restaurants, guide shops, and gas stations to leave them on the checkout counter. Some businesses had a corkboard by the front door. The Lakefront Chalet attracts a lot of fisherman because of the local trout streams, so while fishing, I would strike up conversations with other fishermen. When parting ways I handed them a business card, and told them that I have a great place to rent up here, and that they should consider it for next year. This was a great way to personally connect with a potential renter and pre-screen them.

Charity Auctions

Ever since we have owned vacation rentals, we have offered our places to charity auctions for a free weekend. The charity creates an advertisement for us, e.g. a poster board, and everyone there will read about our property and have the ability to bid on it. It is a great value for the charity and it makes us feel good. Years ago, the people in the charity bid on our place because they liked it so much. That tells the people in the room how great your place is! We obtained a few other rentals from this method because people would talk up the place, and others grew interested and rented from us. In addition, people at charity auctions are probably in your target market. We donated weekend stays at the Lakefront Chalet to a charity that helps terminally ill children fulfill their lifetime wish for a trip in the outdoors. Most people at that auction were outdoor people, exactly the kind of people who would rent our property.

When the winner of the auction contacts us to book their trip, we still require a signed rental agreement and a security deposit. Note that each time we offer our property to a charity auction, we specify black-out dates, and excluded special dates such as holiday weeks and holiday weekends.

Travel Books/Magazines

We used to advertise with Michigan Vacation Guide, a hardcopy travel guide-book for Michigan. At one time they published a yearly book of Michigan travel destinations and lodging. They would actually visit many of the properties in the book, and write up a great explanation on them. We were also featured on their website which, of course, had a link to send readers to our main website. As our repeat business picked up, we stopped paying to advertise through this travel guide.

Niche/Draw

You should think about other non-conventional ways to advertise your rental property. Our Lakefront Chalet is near some of the best trout streams in the Midwest. In addition to advertising with local bait/tackle shops, we met a few local fishing guides, offering a discount to their clients if they stayed at our place. I invited the fishing guides over to look at our place so they knew exactly where their clients were going to stay, and what amenities to expect. We also advertised with bait/tackle shops in the Detroit area, because those shops organize weekend fishing trips to these streams for their customers. We tried out other niche avenues such as Woods-n-Water magazine, local "Bulletin News," and online at www.michigan-sportsman.com. By doing this you are targeting the people you want to rent your place. Over the years we also met other people and business in the area, and mutually agreed to include links to each other's websites.

Send Out the News!

Let all of your friends, co-workers, and family know that you have a vacation property for rent. Mail them a letter, send them an email, post a flyer at work: just make sure they all know about it! If you are involved in any clubs or organizations, post a flyer on their bulletin board, advertise in their newsletter, or make an announcement at their monthly meeting. Why do all this? Well, you have friends and belong to certain clubs. These are people like you, who probably share similar interests and are your peers – people you trust and respect. These are the best renters! You know that they will take good care of your place. Many of my friends offer to do work at my properties because they appreciate the opportunity to vacation there. Put these people in your renter database as well, so they can get your correspondence on special offers and any advertising you send out.

Photos

Take good photos of your property inside and out. I often see pictures of advertised properties with kitchens that have dirty dishes in the sink, or bathrooms with the reflection of the guy taking the picture in the mirror. The best time to take pictures is after the cleaning person has cleaned and straightened up the place.

Leave all your stuff in the car and take ten minutes to snap as many pictures you can. Do this during the day and turn on every light in your house. With a digital camera or your phone, take about ten pictures of every room, and from different angles. Hold the camera above your head and point it down a bit, get on your knees and angle the camera upward. Take a picture from one corner and then the other corner. Do this outside as well; take as many pictures and angles as you can. Then leisurely look through the pictures and show them to whomever you are with; ask their opinion about which images they like and would expect to see on your website.

Your goal is to have enough good pictures loaded on your website to convince a prospective renter to rent your property. You do not have to show every single room in your home, but taking pictures allows you to select the best ones for your advertising.

You will also want three great pictures of your property; one inside, one outside, and the third for the main draw. You will use one of these three as your "calling card" picture. It will appear on the main page of your website, and on all of your print and online advertising.

You can see pictures of all of our properties in the Resources area on getawayx.com.

Social Media, Facebook/Twitter

In the past I did not use Facebook or Twitter for my vacation rental properties, and I currently do not actively use them. However, I have reserved Facebook, Twitter, and YouTube accounts for each of my properties. I reserved them to prevent others from using them. Social Media is discussed in the Website chapter.

Newsletters and Online Blogs

I have never used newsletters or online blogs, and don't intend to use either. Both require your commitment to maintain them for eternity. I have a day job and a family at home; I don't have time to write newsletters and blogs. If you have a monthly newsletter and stop doing it, people will wonder what the heck happened to you. Blogs require a daily commitment. If you really want to do a newsletter, send it once a year and contact your previous renters. When we contact our previous renters, we inform them of updates and upgrades to our property, cross-sell them on our other properties, and add other relevant information. Send your newsletter via email so it is easy and cheap. I know of people in other professions who have sent monthly and quarterly newsletters to their clients; all of them have told me that it is very time consuming and tough to keep up with, and difficult to come up with topics to write about. If you choose either of these methods, think it through and keep it simple.

Other

We use www.vistaprint.com to make pens, writing pads, and refrigerator calendar magnets with our property name, picture, and website on them. We leave a big box of pens and writing pads in our supplies closet. When the cleaning person comes she puts out a few pens and pads on the kitchen counter. People walk off with them, and that is what we want to happen. We want them to take the pen home or to work, and have other people ask about that pen. You can mail these items to previous renters as well. Years ago we mailed refrigerator calendar magnets to all of our previous renters, friends, coworkers, and family. Each magnet showed the yearly calendar, the main picture of our properties, our website addresses, and our phone number.

GetawayX.com

By now you know that there are many ways to advertise. Most of them come with a fee or charge. Even printing business cards and flyers costs a little bit of money for the paper and ink. The advertising for vacation rentals is extremely fragmented, with websites all over the place – there are state-focused sites, national sites, free sites, Craigslist, and so on. Googling "vacation rental" comes up with a gazillion hits. On GetawayX.com we provide a comparable advertising site to the big national websites, but ours is free. You will learn more about the GetawayX.com website in the Website chapter, later in this book.

Chapter Recap

- Your vacation rental business should be run through YOUR website, not anyone else's.
- Marketing to your previous renters should be your first priority. Your goal is to have the majority of your bookings be repeat renters.
- Once again, market to your existing renters and get them rebooked year after year!
- Don't worry about property reviews; many of us are very successful without them.
- Advertise several different ways, and focus on your target market.

Chapter 9

Managing the Property

What you will learn . . .

- How to be a landlord
- The inquiry/rental process

. . . and more!

Management Companies

Management companies are designed to advertise, book renters, collect rent, and clean the property: they do it all. At some locations, however, you must use the onsite rental management company in order to rent your property. I found that out after looking at a condo in northern Michigan. After paying the management fees, the math didn't work out, and it wouldn't have been worth it to me, so I moved on and looked at different properties and developments around that area. Each property owner's situation is unique, and using a management company will depend on your situation and break even numbers.

If you have the choice, I recommend that you manage the property yourself. I prefer to have control over my investment, how it performs, and how it is maintained, rather than leaving it in someone else's hands. I am not saying that a management company will neglect your property; rather, I prefer to control the management process. Management companies typically take 10% to 50% of your collected gross rent, meaning that if they rent your property for a week at $1,500 and charge a 20% management fee, they will take $300 of the $1,500 before any of your expenses (cleaning costs, repairs, and so on). In this example, if your property rented for 20 weeks out of the year, you would pay $6,000 in management fees. Moreover, a 20% fee is reasonable. I know a management company that charges 50%. Clearly, having someone else manage your property can be very costly.

What happens when something goes wrong? Does the management company deal with the situation as you would? When a renter complains, are they bending over backwards to help? When something breaks or needs repair at your property, the management company may recommend options to fix the issue and the costs involved, or they may just do the fix and bill you. When our Ski Condo ceiling caved in, many other units in our association were also affected. We called our contractor, who gave us a quick and cheap option, and the cost to do it the right way. We chose to pay more money and do it the right way, giving us control over who we used to fix the problem. The management company will use "their guy" to do it.

After reading this chapter you should understand how to manage a vacation rental. If you decide not to manage the property yourself, there are many resources available on the internet to help you search for a property manager. The Vacation Rental Managers Association (VRMA) (www.vrma.com) is an international, professional trade association of the vacation rental property management and hospitality industries.

Do It Yourself

Being your own landlord gives you control of your rental property. Ask yourself this question: why would a management company place a renter in your property versus someone else's property they are also managing? Is your property as special to the management company as it is to you? (If your property is the only one they are managing, that is another problem!)

Doing it yourself allows you to control advertising, renter selection, and renter relations. Landlording for a vacation property is much easier than for single-family homes. My wife began with no real estate experience, and she easily manages our vacation properties. The primary goal is to keep your renters happy and get them to rent from you again. She does this better than anyone she could hire – including me!

Now that you have everything set up for your business, your property is ready to be rented. Your advertising is working for you, and the next step is taking reservations and booking. Do not overburden the renter; keep the process quick, simple, and easy for them and for you.

Here is how the process works (see Figure 9.1):

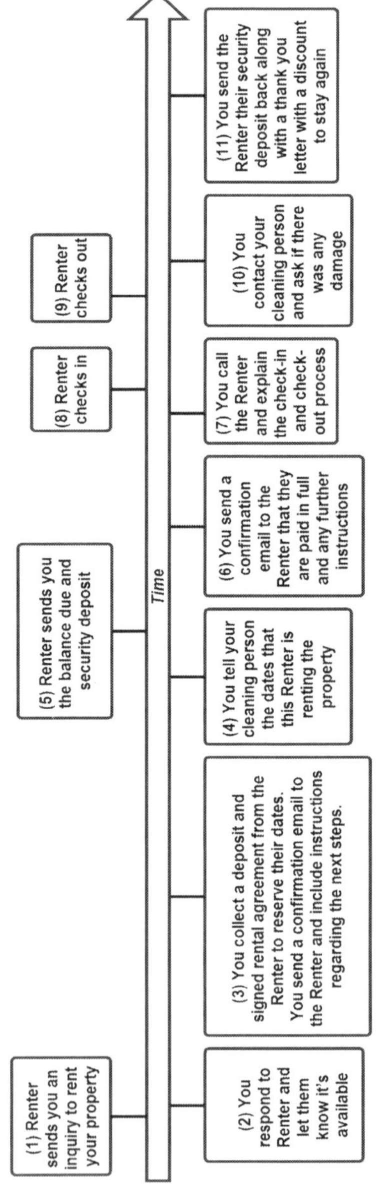

Figure 9.1: How To Book and Rent Your Vacation Property

Your inquiries will come in via phone calls and emails, asking if certain dates are available. If you utilize the tools at GetawayX.com, your inquiries will arrive via the online reservation system on your website. If you have ever searched for and booked a vacation rental, you will know that it takes time to find what you want. But when you find the property you are looking for, you immediately send an email or call the person to book it.

Keep on top of all inquiries and check your email and phone for messages at least once per day. You cannot miss or delay responding to an inquiry because the prospective renter has probably sent the same email to three other people, so get on it quickly. Reply to all inquiries even if your place is not available! They chose to inquire about renting your property over others they have seen, and are a potential renter, now or in the future. Use their first name when responding, and let them know of other available dates. If you are having trouble filling some dates, offer those dates at a discount. Even if the potential client doesn't rent from you, enter their information in your renter database as a prospect.

If your property is available for the requested dates, send them your form email (samples can be found at GetawayX.com) letting them know it is available, how to reserve their dates, and how to send in the deposit that will hold their reservation. If you are using GetawayX.com, you will instruct the renter to reserve the dates and pay you through your custom website. If you choose not to accept online payments, your form email should include the option to pay the deposit via a personal check, along with your physical address.

I require a 20% deposit to book the reservation, and the balance is due three weeks prior to the booking date. It's a good idea to charge the same deposit as your competition.

Sometimes we get email inquiries that say, "Another unit in your complex is $400 cheaper, can you match their price?" Or, "Your place looks great, but our budget is only $500, can you come down in price for us?" These prospects usually explain in detail how clean they are, how well they keep the houses they rent, and what great renters they are. In all my years of renting traditional single-family homes, I have heard that line many times, and have always had to evict these renters. People will try to take advantage of you! Have you personally ever reserved a vacation rental and explained that you are a great renter and how well you take care of things? Of course not!

Unless we are strapped for rentals or it's a last minute booking, we do not adjust our prices. I did a lot of research online and have a very good idea of what we should be able to get in rent. I know that our Ski Condo is the only property with a chair lift right outside our back door; the other guy charging $400 less is probably a couple blocks off the ski hill. Make sure to point out the benefits of your property over the others, and why it is priced the way it is. Remember, the person calling only saw the listings on the internet; they have never personally seen your property or the others they are comparing yours to. More than likely the prospect has sent the same email to five other owners just like you. Don't budge on your prices unless you really have to. If you did your research correctly in the first place, you should be charging an acceptable rent.

If you follow my model, create your website, and put all the recommended information on it, your inquiries will ask if the property is available for rent, not what your rates are, or how many bedrooms there are. I have had many compliments about the content and the detail on my websites, which include facts such as potato peelers in the kitchen. When people call to book our rentals, we ask if they have any questions; 99 percent of the time they say no. That is exactly what you want!

> Screen your renters. You do not have to rent your property to every person who inquires. It's your vacation property that you bought with your money, and are allowing strangers to use.

If an inquiry sounds like a scam, or you are uncomfortable with it, don't rent to them. You can look up the prospective renter on Facebook or Google. We have a maximum occupancy, pet policy, minimum age limit, and other rules. You as the owner will set your own rules, but make sure to stick to them. If a prospective renter asks you to bend your rules, or discount your rent, or change the payment terms, don't do it if you don't want to – hold your ground. In my experience, those who have asked me to bend my rules or change my process have been bad renters.

Taking Reservations

I recommend never using a "Book it Now" button on any of your advertising websites, for two reasons. First and most importantly, your availability calendar will not be updated on all your advertising websites, and letting a renter book your place through an advertising website will cause double bookings on the same dates. It will be a mess. Secondly, the "Book it Now" button might allow the renter to book your property before you have screened them.

> The process of renting and managing your vacation property is nothing like running a hotel.

You are renting out your vacation home, something that you love and want to take care of. You must screen your renters before they book, and they must play by your rules. If a renter clicks a "Book it Now" button and reserves your property on the spot, you lose all control over the reservation process. Keep it simple, and keep all of the reservations on your website. It will make everything much easier for you and the renter.

Your main "availability calendar" must be kept up to date on your website – don't bother with the calendars on your other advertising websites. A main calendar that is completely blank or empty could turn off potential renters. If the main calendar is not updated in a timely fashion, your prospective renters will be annoyed. Not updating your calendar also wastes a lot of your time, telling people that your property is already booked. I am talking about your MAIN availability calendar, the one on your website, not the calendars on the big national advertising websites. I have never updated my availability calendar on advertising websites. I have no idea how to use them, and it doesn't matter. There has been no effect on my rentals, because all my advertising website pages direct clients to my website for the availability calendar, and for booking.

The number one rule is that ONLY ONE PERSON TAKES RESERVATIONS. We learned this the hard way, because twice we had double bookings. A temporary disaster, but we offered each renter a new reservation for free, and one of them always accepted. We lost rent, but didn't lose a repeat renter. This only happened because one of us forgot to mention to the other that the property was booked.

If you are using a GetawayX.com website, an online reservation system is already built in. Keep the reservation process as simple as possible, and avoid the possibility of double bookings: after screening the renter, direct every inquiry to your website, and reserve their dates using the reservation system on your website. You can set up your website to have renters pay the reservation deposit online. Your site is also designed to ask for and track the renter's relevant information, in order to keep track of the dates they reserved. You can get more detailed information on how this process works at GetawayX.com.

If you are not using your website, GetawayX.com, or an automated system to track your reservations, you can do it the "old way" using a physical month-at-a-glance yearly calendar. This calendar allows you to view a whole month at a time, with plenty of room to write in the information you need. Using this method – after screening the renter – tell them to mail you a check for the deposit in order to hold the reservation. Then log the following information in your month-at-a-glance calendar for the dates reserved: the renter's name, address, phone number(s), email, the amount you charged, how much you have received for their deposit, and the balance due.

Next, email the renter a short verification that their deposit has been received, and instructions on when to send in the balance due with the rental agreement. Keep a copy of the email as their confirmation. Note on the calendar when they have paid in full, and when you have called them to explain how to get into the property.

Determine a standard process for when the final payment is due. We ask for final payment three weeks before any scheduled trip, which is customary for our rental area. I have seen owners set the final payment due as little as one week before the trip, and as long as three months before the renter's stay. There are different standards in different rental areas; again, keep in line with how other vacation rentals operate in your area.

Make sure the cleaning person knows the dates being reserved, and when people are coming and going to and from your property. Your cleaning person should be aware of your online availability calendar, but don't expect them to always check it. It is your business to make sure they have a cleaning schedule. Your cleaning person can use the online calendar as a backup.

After the renter sends you the balance due with the security deposit and the signed rental agreement, update your calendar to show they are paid in full. Email the renter acknowledging that the final payment has been received, and that you will call them to discuss check-in procedures and answer any questions they may have.

Calling the Renter

When the renter has paid in full, and has sent you the security deposit and a signed rental agreement, the next step is to call the renter and explain the "check-in" procedures. Here you just provide them with directions to the property, how to open the door, and any other relevant information they need to know regarding their stay at your property. As I mentioned before, do not overburden the renter: keep the process quick, simple, and easy. Unless the renter has a lot of questions, stick to your main check-in list, a sample of which is provided on GetawayX.com. After you go over your check-in procedures, ask if there are any more questions – and that's it. This is the last time you contact them. The next correspondence you will have is after their trip is over, when you return their security deposit.

Do not bother your renters. Do not show up at the property unannounced – ever. Leave them alone to enjoy their vacation.

After Their Stay

After their stay, check with your cleaning person for damage. If you live in the area, check the property yourself. If there was no significant damage, send the deposit check back to the renter along with a thank you letter. In the letter, remind them of the repeat booking discount, and anything else you'd like to tell them. Don't forget to send a thank you letter! They have just left your property, and now is a great time to have them book a repeat trip. If there was damage to the property, follow the security deposit laws in your state when you hold back any of the security deposit funds. There is more discussion regarding security deposits later, as well as in the Legal chapter.

Rental Agreement

I strongly recommend a rental agreement: I have never rented a property without one. The agreement outlines what the property owner expects from the renter, what the renter should expect from the owner, and the rules renters must follow. Each state has different landlord/tenant rental laws, so please contact an attorney in your property's area and draft a rental agreement that complies with your local and state laws. The agreement should be as short or as long as necessary.

Ask other owners around your property for a copy of their rental agreements, and determine if there are other items that should be included in your rental agreement. It is imperative that the renter sign, date, and mail you the rental agreement prior to renting. You can use your GetawayX.com website to accept a signed, online rental agreement, instead of having the renter print, sign, date, and mail/fax it to you. A sample rental agreement can be downloaded in the Resources section at GetawayX.com.

Offering Discounts

Simply put, previous renters get a discount if they rent from me again. I also offer my renters a discount if they refer someone to me who then books a trip. Like-minded people tend to hang out with each other. If I like a previous renter, chances are I will like their friends and family. It's a much better bet than trying to get a completely new renter from an advertising website.

I also offer discounts when I book up and have odd dates left open. The Ski Condo weekends book up fast, but I tend to have mid-week days available. Once the weekends are booked, I offer a discounted rate for mid-week rentals. To everyone who inquires about a date that is booked, I immediately reply that it is not available; however, I tell them of alternative dates that are open, and any dates that have a discounted rate.

> Use discounts to your advantage and come up with ideas that might work in your area. For example, instead of discounted rent, give them a discount coupon to the amusement park near your property. Check out what your competition is doing and try to one-up them.

Taking Payments

Over many years of investing in vacation properties, I have never taken credit cards for rental payments. We have always received payment in the form of personal checks. Personal checks can bounce and you also have to deposit the checks, but depositing has become much easier with smart phone banking apps that scan checks directly into your business account. I am not against taking credit cards, and in fact we are implementing credit card processing on our website. I never took credit cards because I never had to, but I have never lost a renter. However, many people like to pay online, so I believe that you (and I) should offer online credit card payments on your website. If you accept credit cards, however, the renter can dispute the charge and get their money back. In addition, there is a 2% – 5% fee to process the credit card transaction. But the processing fee can easily be passed on to the renter online by charging the renter a processing fee, or by just building the fee into your rental rates.

Taking credit cards should be part of your business model – at least for the initial deposit to reserve your property. The reason to accept the initial deposit via credit card is because there is no delay in getting the reservation booked. It could take a week for them to send you a check to reserve the property, and in that time you will receive more inquires. It does become a little difficult telling people that the date they want is reserved, but that you haven't received the deposit yet and that you will contact them in a week if the dates are still available. After you have swapped correspondence with a prospect and have told them that the date is available, it is much easier for the renter to book their trip and pay their deposit at your website, using your online reservation system.

I use PayPal on my website, but you can use any payment processing link on your website at GetawayX.com. I use PayPal because it is a "payment gateway," which means that I don't collect credit card information. Never take credit card information via email or over the phone. There are strict laws governing how credit card data can be collected and stored, and you could easily violate these laws if you do not know exactly how to do it. Rather, instruct the renter to go to your website and pay there, via the PayPal payment system (or another credit card payment gateway if you choose not to use PayPal).

Cancellation Policy

Draw up a specific cancellation policy for renters to read and agree to. Our policy is that a renter forfeits their deposit if they cancel within three weeks of their stay. I have seen all types of cancellation policies, but your best bet is to follow the other vacation rentals in your area. Search the national advertising sites for rentals like yours in your area, note their policies, and adopt a similar one.

During the past twelve years we have never kept a deposit due to cancellation. There have been a few cancellations but always for good reason. I realize that their excuses could have been complete lies, but I am in the business of keeping my renters and potential renters happy, and to come back again, not to lose them and their friends' business for a few hundred dollars. If you have a couple weeks notice, chances are you will be able to find a new renter by advertising a "special last minute deal."

Think long-term: if a previous renter of yours cancels, I would let them off the hook, or tell them you will apply their deposit to the next trip they book with you. Be reasonable with them!

A few years back we had a January snowmobiling reservation for the Lakefront Chalet. The week before their trip they called and asked if they could cancel because there wasn't any snow on the ground. It made sense: they reserved our place to go snowmobiling, but there wasn't any snow! We didn't even think twice about it; we let them cancel and returned their deposit. They appreciated it so much they immediately re-booked with us for the following year.

> If for some reason you decide to keep a deposit, try offering the renter the option to apply their deposit to a future booking. You want to keep people happy so that they want to stay with you again. Remember that bad press travels faster than good press.

Maximum Occupancy, Minimum Nights Stay, and Minimum Age Policies

Determine how many people your property will hold. This is pretty obvious, but in your advertising people will look to see if their group will fit into your property. There might be local ordinances regarding maximum occupancy. Our minimum stay is two nights, but three-nights minimum for holidays and special weekends. Your best bet is to keep in line with the other vacation rentals in your area. It could be a minimum one-week stay, or even one month. Setting a minimum age policy is a must. We only allow people 25 or older to rent our vacation homes. You want to reduce the chance of property damage, and avoid upsetting your neighbors with unruly renters. All of these items should be included in your online advertising, in your rental agreement, and on your website.

Security Deposits

Don't mismanage your renter's security deposits. There are strict rules governing security deposits in every state, and you must know them. Follow the rules in your state and do not deviate from them.

There are limits on charging security deposits – usually a specific process you must follow to cash a security deposit check – and a specific process to withhold any of the funds for damage. This is a serious topic with serious laws. We only accept personal checks for security deposits, and we do not cash them; rather, we hold the check and shred it, or send it back after their stay if there was no damage.

I would never accept a credit card for a security deposit for two reasons: 1) In Michigan, if you cash or deposit a security deposit, the funds must be held in a separate non-interest-bearing bank account, and not commingled with any of your other money, and 2) the renter can easily dispute the credit card charge and the credit card company will most likely side with the card holder; if that happens you are out of luck, not to mention the damaged relationship between you and the credit card company.

If you have to keep a deposit, you must document what happened, along with photos. Again, know your state laws when holding back security deposit funds.

Things will get broken and damaged, the carpet might get a couple stains here and there, and a spoon might go missing. I do not get bent out of shape about this – it's part of the cost of renting. I choose not to hold back security deposits for these small things; but if the damage is more than $200, I might talk to the renter and find out what happened to get their side of the story – because it is difficult to prove which renter broke what. Sometimes it's best to just fix it and never rent to those people again.

> If a renter damages your property, whether minor or major, you don't have to rent to those people ever again.

We do not require a security deposit for a few special repeat renters. We have gotten to know a lot of our renters really well as they have rented from us for over ten years. We have many trusted repeat renters who tell us about things they fixed for us while they were staying at our place. Just recently one of the repeat renters called me and said that one of their party accidentally broke the crock-pot. He told me they went out and bought a new one and apologized for any inconvenience. This is precisely why you need to leverage your previous renters and turn them into long-term repeat renters you can trust with your property.

Jon talks in detail about security deposits in the Legal chapter of this book.

Renter Complaints and Issues

At some point you will run into issues and complaints, and there will be some people that you just cannot please no matter what you do. Keep in mind that you want to do whatever you can to make your renters happy, and accommodate them. However, this has to be within reason - what a normal, rational person would expect. Your renter has taken time out of their busy schedule to vacation at your property, and you want it to go as smoothly as possible for them. Always listen to them and sympathize with them. Your main goal always is to convert every good renter into a repeat renter.

We had a renter call because she could only find one remote for the three TVs at the condo. In addition, some of the kitchen supplies were missing, making it made hard for her to cook. We called a local restaurant and got a gift certificate for $150 for her family. Dinner was on us for the rest of their stay.

Your renters are your guests, treat them the way you would expect to be treated. Most of the people who had problems with the property have rented from us again because of the way we handled it. Be realistic: some things might not be able to be fixed before they leave, and they will have to deal with it during their stay. In that case, you can refund a percentage of the rent, or accommodate them the way you would want to be accommodated if you were them.

Scams

We have only been approached by a few potential scammers. Scamming typically involves a group or family overseas wanting to rent your place. If the email looks fishy, it probably is. When a legitimate person wants to rent our place the email is like this: "Hi, we are looking to rent your condo Feb 10th–15th, is it available?" Very short and to the point. When you get a request that reads like a book, question the legitimacy of it. Keys to look for: bad English, a formal tone, offering to pay a certain amount now, wrong information (i.e., condo vs. house). Just use common sense, and if the inquiry sounds weird or too good to be true, don't respond to it.

Scamming involves fake money orders, fake cashier's checks, and fake checks. A person could book your vacation rental, send you the deposit, and within a day or so call to cancel and get their deposit back. In this case you probably just deposited their check so it has not had time to clear the bank. If you send one of your checks back to them refunding their money, their bad check will not clear.

Always wait until you have verification from your bank that funds have cleared before sending money back to a renter. This applies to credit cards as well.

If someone books your property and pays the deposit via a credit card, and then promptly cancels the reservation, that would send me a red flag. Tell the renter that refunds are only sent after verification that funds have cleared, and after credit cards have been fully processed.

A request to pay via a bank wire could be a red flag. Wire transfers are more commonplace internationally, but not here in the US. I would question a renter who eagerly wants to send the rental amount via a bank wire. In addition, red flag any inquiry where the person eagerly wants to send you money, especially the entire rental amount, up front. If you were to rent a property to vacation, would YOU want to send all of your money up front, or would you just send them the required deposit? Think logically and remember that you do not have to rent to anyone you feel is fraudulent. The inquiry might be legit, but in all my years of renting I have never had a renter want to prepay the entire rental amount up front, nor have I ever had a request to receive funds via a wire transfer.

Put a rent collection process in place and do not waiver much from it. Many scams ask you to bend your rules, or change the way in which rental monies are sent. YOU dictate the payment options, not the renter. If they do not like your terms, you do not have to rent to them. Every quality renter we have had follows our process, and does what we say with no questions asked.

Keep in mind that scammers call from certain notorious area codes. Beware if you receive a phone call from the following area codes:

- (242) Bahamas
- (246) Barbados
- (264) Anguilla
- (268) Antigua
- (284) British Virgin Islands
- (345) Cayman Islands
- (441) Bermuda
- (473) Grenada
- (649) Turks and Caicos
- (664) Montserrat
- (758) St. Lucia
- (767) Dominica
- (784) St. Vincent & Grenadines
- (809) (829) (849) Dominican Republic
- (868) Trinidad and Tobago
- (876) Jamaica, and
- (869) St. Kitts & Nevis.

A phone call from one of these area codes looks like a United States area code, but it isn't!

Chapter Recap

- You are not a hotel; your rental property is an investment home you have purchased. Screen your renters before allowing them to book your property.
- Inquiries to rent your property will come in via email and phone calls. Be prompt to respond and only have one person in control of the reservation process.
- Discounts can be used to entice people to rent your place off-season, and during odd dates.
- Don't mess with security deposit laws – follow the rules that apply in your state.
- You will get a few renter complaints – you cannot please everyone. Be courteous, but remember, you don't have to ever rent to them again.
- YOU dictate the payment options, not the renter. Stick to your procedures and don't get scammed.

Chapter 10

Accounting

By Gary Herberholz, Certified Public Accountant

What you will learn . . .

- IRS rules for vacation rentals
- Allowable expenses

. . . and more!

This chapter is for informational purposes regarding vacation property accounting, and is based on the year of publication. This is a brief overview of what to expect, but please consult the advice of your own Certified Public Accountant (CPA). I strongly recommend that you find a CPA who has experience dealing with vacation real estate as an investment.

As discussed in previous chapters, traditional investing in real estate is not for the faint of heart. It was perfectly pointed out that residential real estate can be a nightmare. I have been Trevor's CPA throughout his residential investing, and I have used him as an example to my other clients of why it is so difficult. He came up with innovative ways to be a landlord, but also learned that the time wasn't worth the money. During my twenty-plus years doing taxes, I have seen very few successes, but many failures in residential real estate investing. I will never dissuade my clients from chasing their dreams, but I will use my experience to give them a harsh sense of reality. I remember when the stock market was struggling; an engineer client of mine decided that his future was investing in low-income housing in Detroit, as a side business. If you have full time renters, you must be a full-time landlord. It didn't work out too well for him.

> Investing in vacation rental property is vastly different than residential real estate, but the tax laws are very similar. The biggest difference is the personal use portion of the rental property.

IRS Rules

The IRS does not consider property to be rental property if it is used for personal purposes during the year for more than the greater of:

- 14 days, or
- 10% of the total days the property is rented to others at a fair rental price.

A personal day is a day that the property is used by:

- You or any member of your family – grandpa, grandma, mom, dad, brother, sister, son, daughter, grandchildren, your spouse....
- Anyone else who has a financial interest.
- Anyone who uses the property under an agreement to use other property.
- Anyone who uses the property paying less than fair rental price.
- Any days donated to a charity.
- Any days "swapped" with another vacation property owner.

That is quite a list, but the more you rent your vacation property, the more you can use it! In addition, personal days are not days you use the property to make repairs or perform maintenance.

If you use the property for more than the allowed personal days, all is not lost. You still can deduct your expenses against your income, but only up to the amount of your income. You are not allowed to create a tax loss on the property.

If you fall within the personal day parameters, you are allowed to deduct your expenses against your income and create a gain or loss on the property as a rental business.

As discussed in the legal chapter, once you have decided to purchase rental property, you will want to research the taxing entities available in your area. This can vary state-to-state and even city-to-city. In most cases, the Limited Liability Company (LLC) is the preferred entity. LLCs are typically the best entity for appreciating property, and taxation is passed through to the owners to minimize double taxation.

Bookkeeping

After creating the LLC, or other preferred entity, you must maintain separate books and records for the revenues and expenses of your new company. You do not need fancy software or complex processes to do this. Simply follow this book's instructions to open a bank account in the name of the company, deposit all rents collected into the business account, and pay all expenses from the business account. Keep track of the source of every deposit, and what every expense is for. Give all of that information, along with your bank statements, to your accountant at the end of the year.

Assuming the property is rented 14 days or more, all rental income is taxable, but any security deposit held in escrow is not. You are allowed to offset your rental income with certain deductions related to the vacation rental property. An example of allowable expenses could be:

- Advertising. There are many avenues to advertise your property, as discussed in the advertising chapter of this book. Keep track of it all!
- Cleaning. Whether it is your regular cleaning crew or someone to deep-clean your carpets, cleaning expenses can be deducted.
- Management Fees and Commissions. Fees to any agents or management companies to manage your property can be deducted.
- Dues and Association Fees. Any association fees or dues that you are required pay on the property.
- Insurance. As outlined in the chapter on insurance, it is important to have the appropriate insurance on your property.
- Interest. The interest you pay on your mortgage.
- Taxes. Real estate taxes you pay on the property.

- Travel Expenses to Check on the Property. Keep track of your travel expenses and give them to your accountant!
- Utilities. Keep track of all of your utility costs; electric, cable, gas, water, etc.

Keep track of all your property expenses and provide that information to your accountant.

Typically this information would be reported on IRS form Schedule E, which is filed with your personal return. This is the point where things become more difficult, and you should consult with your accountant.

IRS Passive Activity Rules

Rental real estate is considered a passive activity, and there are specific rules that apply to passive losses.

The IRS passive activity rules allow passive losses only to offset passive income, not earned income such as wages. Any excess passive losses would be disallowed in the current year, but you can carry the losses forward to use in the future.

In most cases, there is an IRS exception for deducting losses up to $25,000 per year, if you have active participation in the activity (rental home). The IRS limits losses based upon income restrictions. If you make more than $100,000 ($50,000 if married filing separate), your deduction could be limited or phased out.

One reason for the limitation on losses is because tax losses will generally be the result of depreciation. You are allowed to deduct allowable rental expenses from your rental income, but then you are allowed a depreciation deduction from the purchase of the property. The IRS does not allow you to depreciate the property, or any improvements that add value, for more than one year, so they are deducted over a period of time. In many instances you will have a cash profit, but a tax loss resulting from depreciation.

There are many current and future tax benefits when properly investing in real estate. This is why a key component of investing in real estate must involve an experienced CPA.

Chapter Recap

- IRS rules determine whether your vacation rental qualifies as a vacation rental for tax purposes.
- Keep track of your "personal days" and the days that you rent your vacation property.
- Keep track of all your income and expenses via separate books and records for your rental business.
- Make sure to employ the guidance of a qualified CPA who has experience with vacation rental real estate.

Chapter 11

Website

by Matt Clark, Founder of Waypoint Arts, LLC and Developer of GetawayX.com

What you will learn . . .

- The features and benefits of the www.GetawayX.com website
- Beyond the www.GetawayX.com website

. . . and more!

Today's world is rapidly changing. A major driving force behind our high-paced life is technology, powered by instant communication via the internet. For many, this can often seem intimidating - especially when introduced into areas where people are set in their ways, or who still prefer the more "traditional" methods. This is true for almost anyone, even the tech savvy among us; however, being able to harness the power of the internet into your vacation rental will be a big asset to your success. But what does "technology" actually mean in this context? Even more importantly, how much will it cost you?

Maintenance, cleaning services, and utilities are a "must" for your vacation rental. Perhaps in the eyes of some, having a website is lower on that list, especially for newer owners who are just learning the business. Ensuring that your rental is suitable for occupation is indeed a top goal, but having an online presence should be on your property's priority list as well - and why not?

In the United States today, more than half of all Americans own a smart phone capable of accessing the entire internet. The power of the internet is in one's hand, and can now view your property's online home. Just give that a thought for a moment. Establishing an online presence for your property is essential, and listing with the right website is equally important.

As with every business decision you make, researching your options is one of the first leaps to make in your online rental venture. The field of vacation rental websites is rapidly growing, so asking questions like, "How much will this cost me?" or "Will I have complete control over my listing?" is important, and the answers should definitely factor into your decision.

GetawayX is an alternative that allows you to have complete control over your property's listing, rates, reservations, and more. As the designer and developer of GetawayX.com, I've had both the honor and privilege of creating an easy-to-use website at the direction and lead of this book's main author, Trevor Wisniewski. Take a quick glance at some of the powerful features we've built into GetawayX for property owners:

- Completely free membership for owners, property managers, and renters.
- No limit on how many properties you can add.
- Customizable website template for each property.
- Ability to sell online advertising on your website and generate additional revenue.
- Set your own rates, including nightly, weekend, weekly, monthly, and holiday rates.
- Set minimum-night requirements for each rate.
- No limit on how many photos you can upload for each property.
- Renters can sign up, login, and request reservations through your property's website.
- Rate renters and review other owners' ratings prior to approving new reservations.
- Add, review, and give feedback on contractors.
- Access online GetawayX book resources.

As the owner, you have complete control over your listing with a toolbox of powerful resources, known as the Command Center – your "control panel" to manage and view proprieties, reservations, renters, and contractors. This is where the magic truly begins. If you have one property or own several, the Command Center has the controls you need to help make your online ventures a success. Designed for simplicity and built for complexity, the Command Center is your gateway to renting your vacation home.

GetawayX has been designed to make the setup and maintenance of your listing hassle-free and user-friendly, with all property-related pages centralized in one area. Adding photos, customizing your website, and giving the descriptive touch you desire are only a few clicks away. Let's take a quick look into your rental toolbox:

Set Up & Listing

Upon adding or updating your property, the first option available is the Set Up page. As the name suggests, the main aspects of your property are housed in this area. Information such as your property's physical address, the title that was supplied upon adding your site, occupancy, and suitability are some examples of the "set up" to your new rental. You can define policies regarding children, pets, and smoking policies, along with giving renters-to-be an overview of the bedrooms, bathrooms, kitchen, and dining areas.

Aside from your property's location and attributes are a myriad of attractions, activities, and other local services. After all, you are not just selling the actual building, but the local area as well! You'll be able to select from a long list of various areas of interest that will give potential renters a better insight to your property, using searchable fields that visitors to GetawayX can filter through to find your listing. From skiing to beaches, shopping outlets to live theatres, giving your property the descriptive touch will boost its appeal and marketing potential.

Amenities and Photos

What additional features does your property have? Perhaps a big flat-screen TV with the ultimate cable package, an air hockey table, a grill, or a pool? Canoes or bikes? Through the Command Center, you'll be able to give your renters a full description of all the bells, whistles, and add-ons that will make your property shine. Uploading photos is essential to any profile, and owners have a limitless capability. Truthfully, the only limit is on how many photos you have!

Rates and Fees

The core of the Command Center is the Rates and Fees section of your property, which gives you the ability to set costs. From weekdays to weekends, weekly to monthly, at GetawayX you can easily configure the rental rates for your property, with the date ranges of your choosing. Do you want to charge more during the summer than during the winter, fall, or spring? No problem; you can base your "seasons" on any timeframe you choose. Do you want to charge extra for a holiday stay? A "holiday override" capability allows you to set special rates, even if they overlap with the standard rates you have already added.

Along with defining each night's rate, you'll be able to set the minimum stay requirements, and factor any additional fees and taxes. For example, do you want to add a housekeeping fee? No sweat. Add a 6% tax to the overall reservation? Sure thing! The Rates and Fees page serves as the foundation for your reservation booking system, and gives potential renters insight into your prices prior to reserving through your property's website.

Website and Advertising

Designed to empower the owner, GetawayX gives you the options needed to make your property shine. From photos to maps, activities to availability calendar – your property's online guide will attract visitors with its personalized and easy-to-use website hosted at www.getawayx.com/yourpage, included with each property listed. Most pages will automatically display your property's details based on the information provided through the Command Center. For those who prefer a more hands-on approach, you'll be able to free-form the text on your home page, property guide, referrals page, and a few other areas throughout your site. To add even more flair, choose a "cover photo" for your site's banner, and customize the color options on your site.

Unlike other vacation rental sites, you also have the option to sell online advertisements on your property's website, which can generate additional revenue. Not only is your GetawayX listing free, you could even generate additional income with your website by utilizing Google's AdSense program.

At the core of your site are features for users, or "prospective renters." Your GetawayX website is the gateway that allows prospective renters to request and book their stay directly through your site. The prospect enters their desired arrival, departure, and their party size. They will not only be able to view all your rates on the site, but they will be given an estimated cost prior to booking, based on the requested arrival and departure dates. Of course, they'll first have to create an account or log in to their existing account, which can be done through your property's site. Reservation requests are sent to your inbox and also organized neatly in the Command Center's Reservations section, awaiting your approval.

Reservations and Renters

What do your properties, rates, and renters have in common? Reservations and bookings. The Reservations section of the Command Center unites these three elements of GetawayX into one powerful area. Here, you can view all new and existing reservations, approve or deny requests, and finalize costs. Need to perform a quick search? Easily done. GetawayX.com has been developed to be a user-friendly platform for owners to seamlessly administer these requests.

Upon entering the Reservations section of the Command Center, you'll first see pending (new) reservations and renter feedback requests. Newly received reservations receive a "pending" status, requiring your action to either approve or deny that request. You will be able to view the renter's contact information, reservation history with your properties, and reviews from fellow owners to help you decide whether to approve the reservation. A detailed night-by-night overview will also accompany the reservation, breaking down each day's rate and applicable fees. Because GetawayX empowers the owner, final costs are not given to renters until you've approved the reservation . . . or, simply deny the request.

To approve or not to approve? To assist you with that decision is the renter rating system. At the conclusion of each stay, owners are asked to rate the renter on an up or down vote. Providing additional comments is helpful to fellow owners, especially with those troublesome guests that you might want to avoid. For current and previous renters with whom you'd like to retain a relationship, you'll have complete access to their profiles in the separate renter area of the Command Center.

> Just as with reservations, managing renters should be easy and user-friendly. When a user requests a reservation with one of your properties, they are automatically added to your address book. Having the capability to search through this virtual Rolodex makes it easier to find contact information, reservation history, and the reviews of fellow owners.

Payments

Receiving and sending payments should be done with complete security and peace-of-mind. That's why GetawayX recommends PayPal – a reputable and reliable online payment service, giving users the ability to send money without sharing financial information, and the flexibility to pay using their account balances, bank accounts, or credit cards. PayPal has 137 million active accounts in 193 markets and 26 currencies around the world, processing almost 8 million payments every day. Just like GetawayX, signing-up requires no financial obligation.

GetawayX can assist with your online or traditional payment methods. Built within the Payments section of your Command Center is a great tool for tracking payments received and balances still due. This bookkeeping feature allows owners to retain a full history of payments for each reservation.

Beyond GetawayX

Managing your property's overall brand carries over into the online world as well, and the internet should be viewed as a valuable tool. Just like any marketing campaign, you should attempt to cover the largest audience possible with the resources at hand. From the onset your marketing potential may seem limited, because many of us don't have an advertising budget. Fortunately for the web community, social media serves as a free resource to take your brand to the next level.

"Social media" is a broad term for a variety of social networking websites - online communities where one user can interact with another user in numerous ways. Posting pictures, uploading videos, or simply sending a "Hello" message are just a few examples of social networking. The rest of this chapter will give you a broad overview of using social media as an asset to your vacation rental. GetawayX can help you with your property's online foundation, but what you do next is completely up to you!

If you're unfamiliar or uncomfortable with social media, consider becoming more savvy in this area. Break away from your comfort zone and begin exploring your marketing potential by utilizing these (free!) resources. You don't have to become an expert, but social media can increase your reach into the vacation rental market.

"Why," you ask? Well, would you like to . . .

- Reach out to new or potential renters?

- Connect with your current renters?
- Build an online reputation for your property?
- Start a "buzz" about your property?
- Boost your search engine rating?

Hopefully you said "Yes!" to all of the above. For those uninitiated to the social media world, the thought of budgeting your time for posting pictures or writing messages can seem bothersome, or perhaps even intimidating. After all, most of us don't have time to constantly take and post pictures, or film and upload videos! But it's really not that cumbersome, and understanding the marketing potential of social media should be a driving force to help you get more involved. But first, decide for yourself (1) what will be most conducive to promoting my property, and (2) will I actually have the time and effort? More on the latter in just a moment, but take a few minutes to at least research some of the bigger social media sites and their primary purposes. For example:

- Facebook – Photos, videos, blogs, and apps.
- Twitter – "Microblogging" or short messaging.
- Google+ / YouTube (owned by Google) – Multifunctional / Video sharing.
- Instagram – Photo sharing.
- Pinterest – Photo sharing.

This list consists of just a few that came to mind, and doesn't account for all of your options. There are numerous social media sites you can join; however, the ones listed above are some of the most popular (Facebook alone has over a billion active users!) and should be your first stops on the social networking journey.

The easiest way to begin learning about social media sites is to use them. Begin by picking one or two. Sign up, and start exploring. Like most new users, you'll find that Facebook and Twitter are almost as easy to use as GetawayX - almost. Once you are somewhat familiar with the site(s), use them, and continue to use them. This point cannot be stressed enough – it's called social networking for a reason. Remember, it's not enough just to have a Facebook page, a Twitter account, or other social media accounts. You must use them frequently for their intended purposes - networking and social interactions. Here, you'll build your property's brand to new audiences, taking your marketing campaign to a whole new level.

Posting pictures and interacting with users and renters is important, but what else can enhance your online profile? Social media is really about one thing: renting out your property! There is no specific answer to what postings you should make, but perhaps an example would be appropriate to showcase your marketing potential.

YouTube is one of the most powerful resources for vacation renters.

While many social networking sites can host those your snazzy property photos, YouTube is a free video powerhouse. Imagine the marketing potential when prospective renters are able to take a video tour of your rental. You're able to show off that new pool table, or perhaps some footage of the backyard patio. The possibilities are endless, and so are your video uploads on YouTube.

If you are not a video production professional, don't worry. More than half of all Americans own a smart phone, most likely with a built-in video camera. Some even have built-in video editing programs that can add transitions, special effects, or simply edit the footage. Within minutes, you can quickly record that cozy cottage you just listed on GetawayX.com, or perhaps capture the romance of that beach near your villa. Upload the video directly to YouTube, share it on Facebook, and tweet the link to your followers on Twitter.

> YouTube is just one specific example. This marketing philosophy should apply to each social media site you join. With each social media tool you use, ask yourself, "How can I boost my property's online presence with this site?" You don't have to become an expert in this area, just comfortable enough to use these resources proficiently.

Even after this brief overview of social media's potential for your property, many will still be reluctant to take the next step. Some owners may not have the time or the resources to frequently make videos, or tweet. Life is busy and chaotic; I completely understand, and there's no argument there! Even if you don't plan on using sites like Facebook or Twitter, it's still important to at least grab the username and ensure that your online "brand name" is reserved for later use. Let's use "Up North Getaway" as an example. Take a few moments to snatch the account names on those top sites listed above:

- facebook.com/upnorthgetaway
- twitter.com/upnorthgetaway
- youtube.com/upnorthgetaway
- and so on . . .

At some point you might want to turn that YouTube channel into a great guided tour of your property. Personally, viewing the bedrooms, bathrooms, and overall property is a major selling point toward taking the first leap as a potential renter. At the very least, create an account and reserve the username for your property's brand.

Two important points must be stressed. First, the old saying, "You get out what you put in" applies to social media as well. Interacting with current and new renters is important, and these free assets allow you to post images, videos, and other media to the world without cost. Consider it "free advertising" as you plot out your online marketing strategy. This leads us to the second point: know your audience and engage accordingly.

> Utilizing social media is not a guarantee to success. Unfortunately, too many people quit the networking scene or ignore their Twitter accounts (for example) simply because they sent out a few tweets and saw little or no response. Your content must be both engaging and frequent. Just like renting your property, ask, "What will appeal to new visitors?" The same is true for social media.

Now let's consider two more ideas.

(1) Strengthen your property's brand by purchasing a domain name (i.e., yoursite.com). A web hosting package is not necessary, because GetawayX offers you a free site at getawayx.com/yourpage. You only need a domain name. This personalized domain can "forward" or redirect visitors to your GetawayX site, thereby potentially boosting your website's traffic, increasing your reservations, and leveraging your advertising revenue. This domain name should be woven into your newly founded social media campaign, further customizing your property's image to your specifications. Getting your own domain name is completely optional, and you will need to purchase one through a web hosting company.

> Many web hosting companies offer domain name purchasing. Companies like Bluehost and Dreamhost are great places to begin your search, with both short and long term options. NOTE: Purchasing a domain name is different from buying a web hosting package. If you simply want to forward your domain to your GetawayX site, you do NOT need hosting.

(2) To help bolster your property's brand, consider creating personalized mugs, hats, and apparel for men and women sporting your property's name. Do-it-yourself stores like Zazzle.com allow anyone to easily customize items to sell; adding your new domain name to each item is definitely a great idea. While I personally don't own stock in Zazzle, they've proven themselves to be extremely easy and reliable, offering a wide selection of goods to their customers.

You're now ready.

Your new venture begins at www.getawayx.com/begin. From there, you will be able to harness the power of this free resource and master the world of online vacation renting. Take the advice given above on social media and build on your property's new brand. One will compliment the other quite nicely, and allow you to reach your full potential.

Chapter Recap

- GetawayX.com allows you to have your own property website, and includes tools to help you rent and manage your property.
- "Brand" your property.
- Get a domain name and point it to your website.
- Employ social media to promote your property.

Chapter 12

Your Own Getaway 'X'

I have seen many vacation property owners asking how to hold a security deposit back from a renter, complaining about renters not picking up after themselves, wondering how to keep their property safe from all the people coming in and out, asking about the best lockbox, what's the best check-in procedure, how to deal with finicky renters, where's the best place to advertise, should they take credit card payments or not . . . on and on. These owners are trying to fix the symptoms of their problems, not the root cause of their problems. They are treating their vacation property as a hotel – always looking for someone new to rent from them.

Eventually this mentality will cause problems for you, the owner. Every one of these circumstances can be easily averted by following my process. If you focus on growing your repeat renters year after year – people you have rented to before and trust – you shouldn't have any of these issues. Recall that earlier in this book I mentioned renters from whom we don't even collect security deposits. This is the level of trust you want to achieve with your renters. Also, recall that many of our renters thank ME for allowing them to vacation at our property. This is the situation you are aiming for.

After implementing this real estate investment strategy – if you have followed the advice in this book – you should have vacation property that is set up as a business, properly advertised, with your own brand, identity, and website. If you ever want to sell this property, think about what you have created! Your property would be a plug-and-play package for any vacation rental buyer! You will have a business, PO Box, phone number, email, website, repeat renters, everything the buyer wants and needs to rent the property. The new buyer would be able to generate rental income immediately, making your property much more attractive to potential buyers than those of your competition.

Partners

Are you considering buying a vacation property with a friend or family member? On the surface this might seem like a great idea. The best benefit is that you have two (or more) people on the hook for the mortgage, and sharing the costs associated with the property. You may be able to buy a bigger or nicer place, perhaps that condo on the beach instead of the one a block away. During my first decade of real estate investing I always had partners. It worked out pretty well with the type of investing I was doing. Back then we bought single family homes, fixed them up, and either flipped them or rented them to full-time renters. However, vacation property is different.

I purchased my first vacation property with my father. After this experience, I would recommend not partnering with another family member or friend. We had huge differences in opinions about how to manage, rent, decorate, and furnish the property. Moreover, both families wanted vacation time at the property, which lowered our rental income. We overcame most of these issues, but you probably don't want a vacation rental property to ruin a friendship, or to become disassociated from your family! My wife and I bought out my father after a few years owning the Lakefront Chalet. Of course, part of the agreement was that he could still have at least one week up there whenever he wanted!

The experience with my father was not a bad one; it was just uncomfortable. It wasn't fun, for example, getting myself, my wife, my dad, and my mom to all agree on what color and type of couch to buy. Everyone has their own ideas about what the property should look like.

> If you decide to purchase a property with a partner, I strongly suggest that you put in writing (in your operating agreement, perhaps) how you intend to manage, rent, decorate, and furnish the property. Include the responsibilities of each partner in your property agreement document.

For example, who will track the income and expenses and pay all the bills? Who will handle renter relations and marketing? How will you decide to decorate the property? How will you handle spending money to repair or enhance the property? Discuss these issues with your partner(s) and put it in writing before you sign the dotted line to purchase a property.

Fractional Ownership Properties

Many vacation destinations have properties that allow you to purchase fractional ownership. This means you own the property jointly with others, and most likely these people are complete strangers. It boggles my mind how this works, but apparently it does because fractional ownership still exists. For example, if a property offers you a quarter ownership, you own a quarter interest in the property income and expenses. You could use the property on specific dates, and the property rules will normally set by the majority or the association. This type of investment is not what I have discussed in this book, and will not work using the methods discussed here. Personally, I would not buy a fractional ownership with strangers.

Multiple Properties

There is no reason to stop at buying just one vacation property, but I would caution you to first build your experience for a couple years, and get comfortable with this method of real estate investing, before you buy a bunch of properties. If you live in the vacation area of your property, it will be easier for you to manage it, as well as multiple properties. We bought three completely different properties in three uniquely different areas of Michigan with three different draws. Now we have three places we love to vacation in with our family, and to travel between in the future when we are retired.

If you want to really capitalize on this method of investing, get your system working on one property and then cookie-cutter it, using your experience and methods on a similar property in that area. Our Ski Condo is a great example. It is in a condo complex with very similar units at the base of a ski hill. Even when we are booked up we get tons of requests to rent, and my wife jokes that we could fill up five condos.

Once you have a system down and feel comfortable with it, you can easily duplicate it, but remember my comparison between the Ski Condo and Lakefront Chalet properties? At one property people expect a cleaning fee, bath towels, hand soap, shampoo, coffee, and so on. At the other property, renters don't expect any of that stuff. You should align with what the competition provides and charges in your area, and remember that what you do at one of your properties might not apply to another area. As I have said over and over again, lean on your real estate agent and other local property owners to learn as much as you can about how the area operates.

Well, now it's that time, the time to do it! Use this book and the free online resources you have at your fingertips at GetawayX.com. Start searching online where you want to buy your new vacation home . . . your own Getaway 'X'.

Have fun and good luck!

About the Authors

Trevor Wisniewski, Founder GetawayX

Trevor has been investing in real estate for over two decades, but real estate has never been his main profession – it has been used to invest his money. Over the past 20 years he has started several small businesses, real estate investment businesses, internet based businesses, and a registered Broker Dealer that is a member of the Chicago

Stock Exchange. During that time he had also owned, managed, lease-optioned, and fixed-flipped single-family homes and condos.

Since 1995, Trevor has worked in the finance industry as a managing partner of a broker dealer, a trading software developer, a financial advisor, and a proprietary statistical arbitrage equities and derivatives trader. Trevor has held a Michigan real estate sales license since 2002 and has a Bachelor of Science in Business Administration from Central Michigan University, and a Master of Science in International Securities, Investment and Banking from Reading University, England. He is a certified instructor for financial classes and has held many licenses: Series 7, Series 66, Series 63, Series 55, Real Estate Sales, and Insurance Sales; and a member of the Chicago Board Options Exchange (CBOE).

Jonathan Eadie, Esq., Attorney at Law

Jon is a licensed Attorney and a licensed Mortgage Broker (NMLS #1105751) in the State of Michigan. He has practiced law since 1997, most recently with the Law Office of Jonathan B. Eadie, P.L.L.C., with offices in Farmington Hills, Michigan, and Clinton Township, Michigan, specializing in Real Property and Landlord-Tenant issues, both commercial and residential. In addition, Jon currently serves on the Board of Directors and as an officer of a Michigan non-profit corporation whose primary function is the operation and ownership of student housing. Jon holds a Bachelor of Science degree from Central Michigan University, and a Juris Doctor from the University of Toledo College of Law.

John T. Frye, Jr., Managing Partner of Doeren Mayhew Insurance Group

With over 17 years experience in the finance industry, John is a Managing Partner who oversees the financial operations of the Doeren Mayhew Agency. His responsibilities include financial forecasting, long term strategic planning, mergers/acquisitions, and partnership development. John began his career in the P&C business as a producer for the Wolf Hulbert Company. During this time John was instrumental in developing a property and casualty practice dedicated solely to private equity firms and their portfolio companies. He and his partners also developed a benefits practice focusing on life and health insurance. John graduated with a Bachelor of Science in Engineering from Michigan State University. While attending Michigan State University John played varsity lacrosse and was a Big Ten scholar athlete.

Gary Herberholz, Certified Public Accountant

Gary is a Certified Public Accountant licensed in the State of Michigan. He has a Bachelor of Science in Business Administration from Central Michigan University and has been in private practice since 1989, most recently with the firm of Herberholz & Company P.C. in Southfield, Michigan. Gary specializes in small business and individual tax and consulting services. He is a member of the American Institute of Certified Public Accountants and the Michigan Association of Certified Public Accountants. Gary also serves as an officer and director for two nonprofit organizations specializing in medical research and education.

Sandy Gaulin, Senior Loan Officer

Sandy is a licensed professional loan officer with over 11 years in the mortgage industry. Sandy developed his mortgage skill set while working for several years at one of the nation's top ten lenders, where he achieved "Top Producer" status before joining a prominent and successful regional mortgage bank in the fall of 2008. Prior to becoming a loan officer, he spent 15 years in the automotive sector as a project manager for a Tier 1 supplier, and utilizes the diligence and attention to detail from that experience to insure a satisfying transaction for his clients. A consultative approach to lending is one of the signatures to Sandy's method, and he has developed a loyal clientele through his service and integrity. Many of the real estate agents and financial professionals Sandy works with choose him for their own loans, a testament to his level of service.

Sandy earned a Bachelor's Degree from Central Michigan University in 1988, has been certified as an FHA/VA Loan Officer, and is a licensed Loan Officer in good standing with the State of Michigan and the National Mortgage Lending System.

Matt Clark, Founder of Waypoint Arts, LLC

Matt Clark is the founder of Waypoint Arts, LLC – a web design and development company based in Ann Arbor, Michigan, specializing in original and custom web solutions. Prior to launching his business, Matt built websites for various groups and businesses for the better part of a decade. Waypoint Arts was created in 2012 and is fueled by a passion for entrepreneurship and dedication for great websites and designs.

Along with his current work in web design, Matt is also a member of the broadcast media community, hosting a weekly radio program in southeast Michigan on politics, current events, and culture. He holds a Bachelor of Arts degree from the University of Michigan–Ann Arbor, having also been a web developer for the university during most of his college tenure.

Made in the USA
Charleston, SC
28 July 2014